GOD WILL RIGHT YOUR WRONG TOO

Compiled By

DR. NATASHA BIBBINS

God Will Right Your Wrong Too

Copyright © June 2024

Compiled by Dr. Natasha Bibbins

Published in the United States of America by

ChosenButterflyPublishing LLC

CHOSENBUTTERFLY
PUBLISHING

www.cb-publishing.com

Unless otherwise indicated, all Scripture quotations are taken from the King James Version of the Holy Bible (KJV): KING JAMES VERSION, public domain.

Scripture quotations marked (NASB) taken from the New American Standard Bible®, Copyright © 1960, 1971, 1977, 1995, 2020 by The Lockman Foundation. Used by permission. All rights reserved. www.lockman.org"

Scripture quotations marked (NLT) are taken from the Holy Bible, New Living Translation, copyright © 1996, 2004, 2007, 2013, 2015 by Tyndale House Foundation. Used by permission of Tyndale House Publishers, Inc., Carol Stream, Illinois 60188. All rights reserved.

All rights reserved under International Copyright Law. Contents and/or cover may not be reproduced, distributed, or transmitted in any form or by any means or stored in a database or retrieval system, without the prior written consent of the publisher and/or authors.

ISBN: 978-1-945377-38-9

Printed in the United States of America

June 2024

Table of Contents:

Foreword: I Come This Far by Faith By Michael Bibbins	1
Hope for the Harlot By Carla D. Manuel	7
Let the Lord Lead You By Nyoka Hendricks	27
My Wrong Can Be Made Right By Apostle Denzel Lewis	37
Shattered Innocence: A Girl's Journey through Detroit's Shadows By Tanisha Bowman	51
Overcoming the Darkness of Depression to Becoming a Beacon of Light as a Life Transformation Coach By Dr. Monica Floyd	63
From Pain To Peace By Tanisha Burton-Walker	87
I Made the Vow and God Showed Me How! By Mary Russell-Hankins	99
My Pain to My Purpose By Danyelle Custis	109
There's a Sailor in Town! There's a Sailor in Town By Nicole Lindsay Bryant	117
The Facade of a Preaching Wife By Dr. Natasha Bibbins	129

Foreword: I Come This Far by Faith

Michael Bibbins

The title of the book in itself is powerful; *God Will Right Your Wrong Too!* Just think about one thing that you did, and you thought that life was over for you. I can guarantee that if you do this, you will know that no matter what you have done God never gave up on you. This book will speak to the moments when you've felt utterly defeated, when your mistakes or circumstances seemed so bad that you could have found yourself embarrassed, yet somehow you found the strength to keep going. I invite you to reflect on a time when you thought life was over, when you felt lost in the darkness of your own failures or hardships. Consider this: regardless of what you've done or where you've been, God has never given up on you.

I was born in a house on the Eastern Shore of Virginia but moved to Delaware at only two days old. Of course, my older cousin gave me that information. I always knew that I was different and destined to become somebody, but I just did not know who. I soon found my identity through my love for sports. In high school, it was basketball and track that kept me busy. Yes, I was really good at it!

Fast-forward, I spent time in the Marines, National Guard, and Army, total service time was 30 years. I do not take anything for my journey. It was challenging, but I remember my mother telling me when tough times came to put my armor on. I really did not understand the significance of the armor; I would just say okay. She gave me the Bible verse that I live by today, Ephesians 6:11: "*Put on the whole armour of God, that you may be able to stand against the wiles of the devil.*" It took a lot of praying to get me to where I am today. My life had many twists and turns, but I do not believe God brought me this far to leave me.

I would like to encourage you to keep going through your journey because God is truly faithful. It amazes me how I can say that God is faithful now but when I was going through those dark days in my life, I did not know what faith was. Looking at me on the surface, you would never see the dark times; you would never know that I had developed a sickness that I thought would kill me; you would never know that I was alone, but I thank God that through it all, I survived! Again, I have come this far by faith. God came and turned my entire life around and I am forever grateful.

There's a profound liberation in the moment when we shed the weight of our past failures and embrace the freedom that forgiveness brings. For too long I lived in the shadow of my accomplishments, using them as a shield to hide the scars of my mistakes. But today, on May 3, 2024, I stand before you unburdened, having confronted my past with courage and resolve.

In this moment of clarity, I can sing with genuine conviction, "I am free, praise the Lord, I am free." No longer shackled by the chains of shame or regret, I rejoice in the newfound liberty that courses through my veins. It's as if a heavy burden has been lifted, replaced by an overwhelming sense of renewal and vitality. The chains that once bound me have been shattered, and in their place, I am recharged with a sense of purpose and possibility.

This transformation didn't happen overnight; it was the culmination of a journey marked by repentance and redemption. I faced my failures head-on, refusing to let them define me any longer. And in doing so, I discovered the true meaning of freedom—the freedom to embrace my humanity, flaws and all, and the freedom to walk boldly into the future unencumbered by the ghosts of my past.

As I stand on the threshold of this new chapter, I carry with me the assurance that I am no longer bound by the mistakes of yesterday. Instead, I am propelled forward by the grace of God, guided by His unwavering love and mercy. So let the echoes of my song resound far and wide, a testament to the power of forgiveness and the boundless possibilities that await those who dare to believe I am free, praise the Lord, I am free.

So, as you embark on this journey through the testimonies of my fellow co-authors, I urge you to pause and reflect on your own story. Consider how far you've come, how many mountains you've climbed, how many valleys you've traversed. And know this: if God could rewrite the narrative of my life, if He could break the chains of my past and set me free, then He can surely do the same for you. For there is no sin too great, no circumstance too dire, that His love cannot redeem. As you turn the pages of this book, may you find hope, healing, and the unwavering assurance that *God will right your wrong too.*

Michael's Acknowledgements:

I want to first thank God for gracing me with this opportunity to be here today. I want to thank God for a praying mother, Ethel Virgnia Bibbins (Jenny). I love you and truly miss you down here.

I want to thank my wife, Dr. Natasha Bibbins, for not giving up on me and for praying for me. Prayer truly changes things. Remember, we have "Come this far by Faith."

I want to thank my children, who have always been here for me: Michael II, Shenelle, and Pamela (Pam Pam). You all were my strength. It is because of you all that I fought to stay alive. I love you dearly.

I want to thank my bonus children, Wilniqua and William. I love and appreciate you both. And to a special bonus son William McKee—who reads the Word of God daily with me; who would have known that the Bible would be our favorite pastime?

And a heartfelt thank you to my family, friends, and 203rd Cold Steel Family.

I never would have made it without you all and of course without God.

Last but not least, my Recharge Outreach Ministry Family!

Publisher's Reflection

What a privilege it is to publish Dr. Natasha Bibbins' second installment of "God Will Right Your Wrong." Once again, Dr. Natasha has assembled a remarkable group of ministers who courageously share their testimonies of how the Lord turned negative situations and circumstances in their lives around.

In this volume, you will read 11 compelling stories that I am sure will encourage you, no matter what you are going through or coming out of. Each testimony stands as a powerful reminder that the Lord can still get the glory from your story! These accounts of faith, redemption, and God's transformative power serve as beacons of hope, demonstrating that no situation is beyond His reach.

Presenting "God Will Right Your Wrong Too" is an honor and a blessing. I am confident that this collection will uplift and inspire you to trust in God's unwavering love and mercy.

Ayanna Lynnay, Publisher
ChosenButterfly Publishing

Hope for the Harlot

Carla D. Manuel

Synopsis-

As a child I was brought up in the Church. I was taught everything about God!

Prayer and learning His Word was a must. My grandparents kept me in the Church until I was old enough to find a way not to go. As a teenager I decided to live life on my own terms. I went against all that I was taught growing up in Church. I gave up my innocence and began to live life in the fast lane—hanging out, clubbing, sleeping with different men, having children out of wedlock and just being wild. I made a name for myself, and it wasn't a good one. I was the one they told you to watch your man when she's around. I'm the one they said was a Jezebel. I'm the one they called a whore. I was the one they said wasn't a good mother. I'm the one they said would never amount to anything . I'm the one they said would always be the side piece because no man would wife her.

I went through a lot of pain and the pain led me back to the Church and one Sunday I was crying at the altar and a lady came up to me and began to minister to me and tell me that, "God told Hosea to marry Gomer who was a harlot. So, if Hosea could stay married to an unfaithful wife because God told him to then surely God has a man who will take a changed you. He will love and marry you." That day changed my life. Even though I was so broken I didn't believe it at the time, it stayed with me and as I began to mature and try to live more for Christ, well ... let's just say she was right. I want to share with you that there is nothing too hard for God. God will take the least likely and make them likely. **2 Corinthians 5:17:** Therefore if any man be in Christ, he is a new creature: old things are passed away; behold, all things are become new.

Only God can turn a "*whore*" into a housewife. There is hope in Jesus Christ. Ask me how I know. God did it for me. Here is a part of my story.

God Is Hope!

In the beginning was the Word

I was born into a family of two strong praying grandmothers. Having the two of them was my saving grace. The foundation was laid before me. I was trained up in the Lord. Church was every Sunday and prayer was daily. We learned and memorized the Word of God even though we didn't understand it. Church was fun for me. I wasn't actively listening to anything the preacher said, but it was a place to meet my friends and cousins, sing the songs of Zion and dance in joy.

I couldn't wait to get to church and play with girlfriends, pass notes, and talk about the boys we liked and what man we were going to marry when we got older. It was fun and games to me, but what I didn't know was that my grandparents were way wiser than me. They knew that no matter what, as long as I was there in the church the Word would do what it is meant to do, which is permeate.

Even when I wasn't paying attention, I was reciting what the preacher was preaching.

This went on for many years and eventually I became a teen. When I became a teenager, church became less and boys became more. I wanted to stay away from church and stay home to let the boys chase me. I smelled myself and thought I was grown, as my grandmother would say. I began acting out. Being smart lipped. Being sassy and being disobedient. I became very promiscuous. I began to do sexual things for attention and money. Listen, I was blessed to be tall and shapely. I was full of confidence and was unapologetically loose with my goods.

I was never one to care what you thought and I definitely was not offended by anything negative you had to say. It was me and it was my world and I was doing things my way!

I was determined to live life on my terms. I totally disregarded all that I was taught and all that I knew.

The Word tells us, "Train up a child in the way he should go." I was trained up, but I was young. God made provision because He knew it would take some living life and some pain and maturing, age and wisdom to get to the scriptures ending "and when he is old, he will not depart from it." Don't miss that. God knew us and allowed us time. Even in my mess God made provision. **The Word is Hope!**

Promiscuous Girl

It started around the age of 12. I became infatuated with boys and men. I didn't like my appearance. I was at an awkward stage—tall, skinny and I had a long neck. Now, in today's world that's model material, but back then it was not the look. I didn't think I was as cute and developed as most girls my age and that showed in the way I presented myself to boys.

All of the values and morals that my grandparents taught me went out the window. I was very sneaky. The first guy I called my little boyfriend caused my mother to beat me down. He was at my grandfather's house and when he was about to go home, I stuck him out and kissed him on the lip. I thought nobody saw me, but there was my nosey aunt who saw everything. She told my mom and, well, let's just say she laid hands on me right in front of the boy. I was laid out prostrate on the floor and not by the Holy Spirit either. Lord I was crying, and he was crying. He wanted to save me, but he couldn't. So, he did what he knew to do and that was to take off running because he knew he would probably be next.

While this is funny, I now realize something happened to me. That feeling of a man loving me and crying with me and wanting to protect me caused me to feel something. What was it? That was new. That feeling was something that would be a driving force that would navigate the majority of my life up to the age of 28. It was like the stories I hear from drug addicts. You are constantly chasing that first high. Well, I was constantly chasing the feeling I got from that first male. It would lead to a trail of men, sex and lies. I was really searching for that feeling of a man being vulnerable enough to cry for and with me. To stay and try to protect me and love me. This led me down the rabbit hole of man after man after man. I couldn't keep a man because I was acting like the man. I was loving them and leaving them. Then, when I would try to be faithful, they would cheat on me and eventually I would go back to being that person who was messing around with whomever I pleased.

The more I aged the better my body began to look. I was tall and shaped like a brickhouse.

Surely you couldn't tell me anything. I walked in every room with the attitude commanding attention. Women were running my name into the ground, they destroyed my name, and as I walked past them they would be looking at me with frowns on their faces. That didn't bother me at all. I was not easily offended. I had a tactic, and it was simply, "You talk about me and I will sleep with your man or husband." Yes, you read it right and I felt like I was big and bad enough to do it. **Somebody thank God for change.**

Now, what these women didn't know is that even in my mess I had a beautiful spirit. I was funny, kind, smart, caring, giving, and easy to converse with. But more importantly than that, I would discuss my hopes and dreams with others and allow them to do the same. Before we would depart God always came up. Whether it was my faith, their faith, their nonbelief in God or just prayer, we never missed a moment to talk about God. Even in the midst of doing wrong, God was still covering me because He had a plan for my life.

I was taught about God, I was always convicted. Eventually I knew I would stop; it was just the season I was in. Ecclesiastes 3: 1 "***To everything there is a season, and a time to every purpose under the heaven.***" (In season and out of season there is hope in Christ.)

Church Gone Wrong

Eventually seasons change. Once you know God, a change has to take place. This doesn't mean that you will be perfect or get everything right. But that still small voice, the guilty feeling, the sense that that something doesn't feel right is the Holy Spirit. God never leaves us. Yes, even in our mess HE IS THERE! I came to point in my life where I was tired of clubbing ,running men not being a good mother to my children . So, I decided to go back to church. I heard everybody talking about this church and that the pastor was anointed. So, I went to that church. Wow … it was amazing. That place was on fire for the Lord. That pastor was a preaching/teaching man of God. The people there were so welcoming and kind. They showed me the love of Christ. I returned Sunday after Sunday, and I was enjoying the Word of God and a change was taking place in my life. I started to live my life for God. Church became my new life. Everything was about church and I loved it. I was there faithfully and excited. I gave my life to the Lord and accepted Salvation and I was on FIRE for the Lord.

Yep, you guessed it, in the beginning I was running for my life. I was attending a "new members" class with one of my friends and just like that I allowed the enemy to come in. As we know, the enemy won't try anything new, he only comes with what is familiar. Well, I felt like the minister who was teaching was watching me, but not like a look of teaching and training, but a lustful watch. My feelings were not wrong. Soon after a few private conversations what was in me came out and before I knew it, we were in an entanglement. Jesus Help Me, Please!

My flesh was fighting against my spirit. I was at war with myself. The Apostle Paul told us in the Word that "when I would do good, evil is present with me." I was not thinking about the Word, I wanted what I wanted. Needless to say, the word got out around the church that I had slept with the man. The pastor shamed me in front of the entire church congregation and put me out of the church. He told them I was a Jezebel and a harlot and that his minister had done nothing wrong. As expected, a lot of the church members stopped dealing with me too. I was so heartbroken. I know what I did was wrong, and I was OK with being chastised, but why in front of the church?

Why was he only shaming me?

Why did the members leave me out there alone?

Why did his minister get to stay?

More importantly, why was God letting this happen to me?

Even though I had brought this on myself I thought the church would help me and not just throw me away. I had always been bold about whatever I was doing so I was not easily embarrassed or offended. Even though he shamed me I didn't feel ashamed. I did what I did and I meant to do what I did. It was not a mistake. I committed the act willingly. I was not a victim. I just didn't understand why this pastor that I thought loved God and loved his members would just throw only me away.

My favorite cousin, who was a member of the church too, kept praying for me and telling me to never give up on God. God was still God and He still loved me. She told me to repent and pray and ask God for the answers to my questions. Only God could answer me. So, I prayed and got deeper into my words. God begin to reveal that He is God all by Himself. He revealed I was idolizing the pastor and the church as a whole. He revealed that I was not strong enough in HIM to fight off the enemy. I had gone to church looking for God, but I had got caught up in man again. Can I just say this event would have caused most people to leave God and never go back to church? But not me. I wanted a relationship with God and I wanted to be different. I knew only God could change me. I had to keep trying to seek God. I wanted to be found.

1 Chronicles 28:9: *"Know thou the God of thy father, and serve him with a perfect heart and with a willing mind: for the LORD searcheth all hearts and understandeth all the imaginations of the thoughts. If thou seek him, he will be found of thee; but if thou forsake him, he will cast thee off forever."* (Even when it goes wrong our Hope in God makes it alright.)

Who Am I?

I eventually found a new church home and tried my best to live a different life. I kept praying and stayed in my word. I would always reflect. One day, I was sitting at home thinking about how all my life I had been called different names for different reasons. I stopped reflecting and began to pray. After I prayed it came to me. As a little girl I was called DeeDee because of my middle name. It didn't stick. Teenage years I was called Skinny and Ms. Bowlegs because it was a description of my body. Didn't like either of them. Eventually, because of my promiscuousness, I would be called a "whore", a slut, and a trick—*Lord, I needed you more than I knew.*

Then there was a mother and her son in my hometown of Onancock, Virginia who gave me these names; the mother called me Twister because when I walked up and down the street I would walk seductively. Her son gave me the name Slim Goody, which became my moniker. This name stuck with me and the men loved to call me this and I loved it when they called me this. Then there was the church folk, who called me Jezebel and harlot. My parents named me Carla and as I was reflecting that's when I began to ask God what He called me. In that moment I cried and cried because it was not a good feeling to be called bad names and have the bad conversations about those names floating around. God said, "I knew you before you were formed in your mother's womb. You are fearfully and wonderfully made. Listen, it's not what they call you, it's what you answer to." So, reader, remember God's Word. You were created in HIS image. God is love and He loves you. You are valuable, you are precious in His eyes, and God loves you. You are His Masterpiece and His Treasure. In God you are forgiven. In Him we have redemption. But most of all in God you are free. Who the Son sets free is free indeed! I am only who God says I Am!

John 8:36: *"If the Son therefore shall make you free, ye shall be free indeed."* (The Great I Am is Hope.) God was still working it out for me, my future was being prepared.

Worthy

A lot of the time I was striving to be well known when I should have been striving to be worth knowing. Now, the irony in this is that most of the men I slept with knew I was worthy of knowing. They would often say things to me like, "I didn't know you were that smart," "I didn't know you could cook," "I didn't know you listened to me," "I didn't know you were so kind," "I didn't know you were this funny," "You are such a great person," "I didn't know you knew about God," "I didn't know you knew how to pray," "You read the Bible, Carla?" "Wow, you are everything a man would want." But because I presented them with my body so freely, they also had the thought in their mind that I was just another notch on their belt. They couldn't take up time with or settle down with the town's loose woman. Truth is had it not been for God protecting some of you ladies or these men worrying about what others would say, some of you would have been man-less. I don't say this to brag. I say this in the humblest way.

Think about it ... most of them had women already, yet they would risk it all to see me. I know you think it was all about the sex, but, trust me, it wasn't just about sex.

Most women thought men flocked to me for my body. Well, they did at first, but they soon learned it was much more to me than sex. The young me used to think sex could keep a man, but what I realized was that they enjoyed my company, my loyalty, and they felt safe with me.

They felt safe enough to share all that they couldn't with others. What men loved about me was their freedom. They were free to be them. No judgment. Free to explore themselves mentally, spiritually and physically. They would often talk with me about how they wished they had met me earlier in life or how they wished they could take time with me to help me become all that I desired to be. But no one did. No one felt I was worthy enough.

The Truth of the Matter

I was just a young girl who strayed away from God and what her elders taught her. Born to two young parents who were not ready to raise a child because they were children themselves. Traumatized from not having my father around and being bounced from place to place even if my young self had been the one asking to go. I didn't think I was worthy. So, if you don't think you are worthy you will treat yourself like you are not worthy. That's just what I was doing. Selling myself short. Taking the scraps. Eventually I got back into the Word of God and God began to minister to me: "You are fearfully and wonderfully made; you are Precious to Me. Come unto me and let me change your childish thinking because you belong to me." A change came over me. 1 Corinthians:13:11 says, "When I was a child, I spake as a child, I understood as a child, I thought as a child: but when I became a man, I put away childish things." (Hope through God's Redemption)

It Was Necessary

Psalms 51:8 says, *"Teach me to know gladness that the bone that thou have broken may rejoice."* You see when God shows us our sins, it is very painful. I was already convicted of my sins, and I had to look at myself, but when the Holy Spirit started to convict me, it broke me emotionally. I was weak. I cried for days, and I asked God for forgiveness. It was the cleansing I needed. I decided I wanted to be different, so I strived every day to live better.

Soon after, I would meet a new man. I met him while he was visiting his mother's home. I inquired about him but was told he had a girlfriend, so I left the conversation alone. Now, before I wouldn't have cared. I would shoot my shot. But now I was different. God was with me. Later that week, my cousin told me that he had inquired about me and wanted to contact me and she gave him my number. Now I am thinking, *What are you doing, Carla? He has a girlfriend.* I had prayed for God to send me a man just for me, not somebody else's man again. I left the situation alone and he eventually called at 5:30 a.m. (Red Flag). But I answered. This conversation would lead to him telling me he was transitioning out of the relationship he was in. He also let me know he was not ready for another relationship either.

Now, he was 11 years older than me and much wiser than I was. He had heard all the rumors about the fast-moving hot-tail girl I had been, and he was looking to score. But what he didn't know was that things weren't going to go as he had planned. *Even in your mess God will protect you and cover you so that He can get the glory from your story.* This man had planned to have sex with me on our first date and never look back. Now, it could have happened because even though I was in a different place I was still weak. But God had a ram in the bush. The same cousin who gave him my number also called and warned me not to sleep with him. She said that's what the talk was before he left the house to come see me. It was said that I was an easy lady. Well, not that night … I held back. That one night of holding back changed my life. Long story short (because trust me it's a long story with ebbs and flows and highs and lows, but God….) this same man would take the time with me and help me develop as a mother and a woman. Five years later, he would make me his **WIFE!**

Let me testify. Difficulty, adversity, trials, and tribulation were necessary to help me develop and grow in my faith and a closer walk with God. Have you noticed that God uses mightily those who have been broken? No matter what you have done in your life God is able to change, heal and restore. Yes, people will continue to throw up your past, but just know that in Christ, you are brand new. Do not look back. Keep pressing forward. Shame on them if they miss the blessings of the new you. It is my prayer that my testimony will give you hope. God is faithful! It doesn't matter where you start but where you finish. Exceptional things and great comebacks come through exceptionally crushing circumstances. The song writers wrote the song called "I'm Living Proof".

I'm Living Proof

Of what the mercy of God can do

If you knew me then

You'd believe me now

He turned my whole life upside down

Took the old and He made it new

That's just what the mercy of God can do.

God has given me way more than I deserve.

I deserved nothing and He gave me everything!

When you build your hope on things Eternal (God)

You will win.

Who says you can't turn who the world refers to as a whore into a housewife? Well, whoever said it doesn't know God. God can do anything and everything but fail. God changed me! Be encouraged; God can change you too. I wouldn't take anything for my journey. I still had hope. Through it all, I never lost my faith or my hope! God was righting my wrongs all the time!

Endure

I am not telling you that the journey with God is going to be easy or a cake walk. You will suffer some things like guilt, loneliness, persecution, lies, heartbreak, affliction, and pain. But if you learn how to suffer through your walk with Christ the journey will be well worth the glory in the end.

The Word of God tells us in Romans 8:18 KJV, *"For I reckon that the sufferings of this present time are not worthy to be compared with the glory which shall be revealed in us."* Just stay in the Word of God. Pray without ceasing and God will keep you. Don't worry about what people say. They will try to keep you in your past. They will try to make you feel unworthy. People will try to hold you where they knew you used to be. But don't you dare give up. Keep pressing toward the mark of the high calling, which is in Christ Jesus. Let them know you have elevated!

If you are feeling bad about your past sin just know we serve a God that is no respecter of persons. In fact, God has always taken the least likely and made them likely. You would be surprised at the number of people who have done the same thing you used to do but they were sneaky about it. Yep, there will be folk who esteem themselves above you because they think no one knows about their sin /sins ... ahhhh, but they would be surprised to know somebody knows and, more importantly, God knows. The scrutiny you have withstood and will have to withstand over time has prepared you for your journey with God. God has equipped you to be able to stand against the wiles of the enemy. Just don't give up. The race is not given to the swift but to he who endures until the end!

Hold on....

So, queens, hold your heads up; don't mourn your past anymore. God has appointed unto them that mourn to give unto them beauty for ashes, the oil of joy for mourning, the garment of praise for the spirit of heaviness that they might be called trees of righteousness, the planting of the Lord, that He might be glorified. Endure hardness as a soldier because God is righting your wrong too! Why? Because you too are WORTHY! Thank you, Jesus, hope is redeemed! I have been redeemed!

Carla's Acknowledgements

God—who knew me before I was formed in my mother's womb. Whose grace, mercy and unconditional love sustain me. The head of my life. The ONLY ONE who reigns supreme in my world. I want to thank you, God, for everything.

My Husband—Rickey Manuel

The one God kept for me until it was time. God used you to help me become a better Woman, Mother and Wife. You took what others thought wasn't worthy and made my worth far above diamonds and rubies. I'm everything I am because you love me.

My Parents

Vincent Smith and Rebecca Collins—without you there would be no me. I love you with my whole heart.

My Grandparents /Aunt:

Ruth L Custis, Fannie Naomi (Mymee) Smith, Lillie Mae Collins and McKinley Collins Sr. and Aunt Marva J Stanley. My Foundation - My Root - My very present help in my time of need.

You taught me about the most important thing in life—God.

My Children

Brandon, Rickia, Rodneyka (Muffin), Yahzmeen and Zion. I love you all with my whole heart and there is nothing you can do about it. No matter what, my love will NEVER change. Thanks to my 13 grandchildren.

To My Son in Heaven:

TaNie Shaheed Kees, you are missed beyond measure. Continue to watch over your mommy.

My Sister Catina Feaster and Cousin Karen Teagle

Thanks for keeping me grounded and our daily talks are the highlight of my day. I love you both with my whole heart.

My #1 Cousin Tyjuana Harmon—thanks for your unwavering love and defense of me. You are always going to tell me the truth and you always see the good in me. Your prayers are powerful and always needed. My biggest supporter, Thanks for staying true. I have a treasure in you.

My Cousin Ava Gabrielle Wise

Thanks for Bible study teaching/learning God's word with me. Our self-evaluation therapy is very necessary .You are my truth teller. Thanks for always making me go to the root and correct. Your friendship is cherished and You are valuable.

My PPP Posse: You all are my ride or dies! Prayer warriors and a very present help in my time of need. I love you all.

My BC Crew and My 2 Royal Wives Thanks for the safety and no judgment. I love you all.

My Family and Friends : Tashie (Tiki) Smith, William (Bobo) Smith, My Smith, Collins, Pettyjohn and Manuel Family and all my Friends (to many to name) I love you all. Thanks for the daily talks and encouraging words but most of all your prayers.

Last but not least, my sister from the beginning, **Dr. Natasha Bibbins!** Thanks for giving me this opportunity! You are determined to take me with you on this journey. You thought I didn't know, but God revealed it to me. I love you!

Carla D. Manuel

Is the daughter of Vincent Smith and Rebecca Collins. She was born on the beautiful Eastern Shore of Virginia in a little city called Painter.

She has been the wife of one man for over 21 years but together for over 26 years with her King Rickey Manuel. She is the mother of six children, Brandon, Rickia, Rodneyka (Muffin), Ta-Nie (RIP), Yahzmeen and Zion. She is Nana to 13 grandchildren, Remi, Samir, Kasai, Khasheem,

Khyzavion, Jake, Chosen (RIP), Zoey, Liam, Noah, Milani (Baby Manuel) and Chance. Carla holds a BA in Theology and in August of 2020 received her license to officiate marriages. She is a notary, and she started a group on Facebook for parents who have lost children called **Hearts in Heaven**.

Carla's Favorite Scripture is **2 Corinthians 5:17**: *Therefore if any man be in Christ, he is a new creature: old things are passed* *away; behold, all things are become new.* She is living proof that God can change anybody!

Contact Info

Name: Carla Manuel
Email: cmanuel630@gmail.com
Facebook: Carla Manuel
Instagram: 2ThyOwnSelfBTrue
X: 2ThyOwnSlfBTrue

Let the Lord Lead You

Nyoka Hendricks

"A man's heart deviseth his way: but the Lord Directeth his steps."
Proverbs 16:9 KJV

Synopsis

Nyoka explains how God Will Right Your Wrong applies to her life. She got married at 18 years of age while still in high school and was warned many times by friends and family not to marry her high school sweetheart. Despite being told not to do it by the Holy Spirit she gets married anyway! She grew up in church pretty much all her life; she accepted Christ at a young age but still was disobedient to the Holy Spirit despite several warnings. She always did what she wanted for her life and not the guidance of the Holy Spirit, which caused her a lot of pain and grief! Nyoka's story encourages others to obey the Holy Spirit despite what their heart desires!

Let the Lord Lead You!

I decided to devise a plan for my life at 18 years old. I was still in high school and thought I had met my soulmate. He was my high school sweetheart. We dated for a couple of years and a few months later, I got married despite my loved ones telling me not to do it. More importantly I didn't follow the lead of the Holy Spirit. The day of my wedding, as I was preparing my things for the ceremony, a strong feeling came over me and something within me kept saying, "Nyoka, don't do it!" I pondered on it all day; my best man backed out! I left to go pick up my flowers and when I arrived, my fiancé, the pastor, my friends and family were all there and I wasn't dressed. I immediately got dressed against the Holy Spirit and moved forward with the marriage. My life from that point was in shambles. The young man became abusive both verbally and physically. I was stabbed and had a gun put to my head. I was beat up my entire nine months of pregnancy. I went through this cycle for the next 14 years. God kept my life as well as my unborn child's life. He made a way of escape for us. I have always been strong-willed; despite telling me no, I would do what I wanted. I thank God for His hands of protection. God proved to Isaiah 54:17A "No weapon formed against me shall prosper."

"Fear thou not; for I am with thee: be not dismayed; for I am thy God: I will strengthen thee; yea I will uphold thee with the right hand of my righteousness" Isaiah 41:10 KJV.

Repeating Cycles

I found myself married again this time for 11 years and it ended due to infidelity. I do want to say my spouse at the time was also a minister, the pastor, the armor bearer, Sunday school teacher and an usher. I never saw this coming! This hurt so bad as I was sat down from my duties as a minister; I was told it was because I was angry God couldn't use me. At this point I had been married for half of my life and still didn't have a spouse. Time goes on and I think I'm going through healing; at this point I've been single for seven years.

I then met a man who went to church pretty much all his life, his parents were both pastors of a church. We decided to get married after dating for about six months.

This young man was the apple of my eye. I was in love. He had wooed me! This man showed me the utmost love and respect; of course, that was until we were married. He started to change the second night after we were married. I was totally blown away. This man had not disrespected me in any way. He was a gentleman while we were dating. I was appalled; I thought to myself, *What's happening?* That was the beginning of the downfall. I was sure I had married the man of my dreams this time and we would be together until death do us part. I had stayed single for seven years working on me, so I was healed and whole when I got into my next relationship.

Four months after our marriage, I had to leave because of the verbal, mental and emotional abuse. I continued to support my husband. We decided to go through counseling and I went back after six months. Once I returned home, he refused to go back to counseling. There were times when his father would come over and counsel us. The support and resources were there.

Unfortunately, things got worse than they were before! There were a few times when I feared for my life! I really wanted my marriage to work; however, I knew at this point I needed to leave again. I started to look for a place of my own to move but didn't have any luck finding anything. I continued to go through the process as I trusted in God; there were times when it would get so bad I would check into a hotel for the night to get some peace.

In the midst of all of this I contracted COVID 19. When I told him, he started making arrangements to stay away from home; however, his father told him not to because I was his wife and needed him, so he decided to come home. Because he had been exposed, he got tested and he was also positive, although he was asymptomatic. My COVID affected my breathing; my doctor wanted me to go to the hospital as I was very short of breath with exertion. He helped take care of me for a few days. He feels better in about a week and at this point he wants to hang out with his friends. I stayed sick for about a month; he fusses because he wants to bring his children over and I'm trying to explain the house needs to be cleaned and disinfected. That doesn't matter; he wants what he wants and since I'm not in agreement because I want to protect the children, I am such a bad person. He called around complaining to everyone that I wouldn't go get retested so the kids could come for the weekend. He did get them for the weekend despite me still being really ill. He was furious that I didn't do what he asked. I tried explaining I was still really sick; however' it was his way or the highway, so the rage began!

"Behold, I will do a new thing; now it shall spring forth; shall you not know it? I will even make a way in the wilderness, and rivers in the desert." Isaiah 43:19 KJV

God Made a Way!

I continued to search for a place to move into. I was still having trouble. One morning, I got a call from one of my friends. I called her back when I woke up. I didn't get her, so I left a message. She called back and was like "Ny, you called me?" I told her I was returning her call. She said, "Ny, I didn't call you." I assured her I had received a call from her, so we just chalked it up as a mistake. We started to talk and to get caught up. She asked how married life was and I began to tell her. She was shocked and said, "Ny, you don't deserve that." I was in agreement and told her I was planning on leaving as soon as I found a place to rent.

We continued to talk and catch up on our lives and she suddenly said, "Ny, I have a place that's empty." She said, "Get your things and come today!" I explained to her I was still at work and had patients to see that day. I told her I would have to gather a few friends to help me and to rent a U-Haul truck. We both believed the call was not coincident but was a call orchestrated by the Holy Spirit! God had once again made a way of escape. It was sudden! I had once again overridden the Holy Spirit! I prayed about it; however, God did not answer me and I still chose to move forward. I made a choice to try yet again to fulfill my own selfish desires. Although I had put myself in this situation God still made a way of escape, just like he parted the Red Sea and made an escape for the children of Israel. God is so faithful; He will never leave you or forsake you! He was there all the time and He protected me yet again!

"Trust in the Lord with all thine heart and lean not unto thine own understanding. In all thy ways acknowledge him and he shall direct your paths." Proverb 3:5 6 KJV

It Is Finished!

I have disobeyed the Holy Spirit too many times and had to go through pain and suffering that probably would have been avoided had I listened to the Holy Spirit! I will have faith that God knows the plans He has for me, and His plans are to give me hope and a future! When I tried to make my own plans for my life, it failed every time! God had to rescue me from the wrong I had done once again! I have learned to let go and let God no matter what the situation is! I have gotten out of position every time I went through a storm; but I'm serving the devil notice. **It is finished**!

I will not get out of position again! The soldier, even though he's wounded, stays in position! The football player may be hurt, but he stays in position, even if he has to limp! I was distracted by the cares of this world. I will no longer override the Holy Spirit. Disobedience is sin! I realize obedience is better than sacrifice. I will trust in the Lord! Storms come, but they are not to break us, they are to strengthen our faith! Peter was walking on the water without fear until he saw the boisterous winds around him; then he stopped and began to sink. Jesus immediately caught him! If we keep our eyes on Jesus even through the storms of life, He got us! If we fall, He will reach down and pick you up! God will never leave us or forsake us!

Ladies and gentlemen, please wait on the Lord if you are praying for a spouse. If God doesn't answer you when you ask if he/she is the spouse for you, please don't move forward with any relationship until God gives you a yes! This also pertains to friendships, jobs, relocations, every choice you have to make! "Trust God! They that wait upon the Lord shall renew their strength; they shall mount up with wings as eagles; they shall run, and not be weary; and they shall walk and not faint." Isaiah 40:31 KJV

Nyoka's Acknowledgements

I would like to thank my Heavenly Father for giving me life! My parents Pastor Hattie Reid, Deacon Charlie Reid, Brenda and Calvin Lee Ames. My children Fred, Breona, and Joshua.

My Pastors Dr. Natasha and Michael Bibbins of Recharge Outreach Ministries in Virginia Beach, VA.

Dr. Nancy Jones of New Ministries Inc in Dover, DE.

I want to say thank you all for your love and patience as I journey down this road of salvation.

Thank you for trusting the God in me and allowing me to walk out my journey without any judgment. I love each and every one of you and may God bless you all tremendously.

Nyoka Hendricks

Evangelist Nyoka Hendricks is an anointed woman of God who ministers the Word with authority and power of God. Her objective is to share the message of hope and faith to help heal the brokenhearted and encourage them to live under God's covenant.

She currently attends Recharge Outreach Ministry Church in Virginia Beach, VA under the leadership of Pastors Dr. Natasha and Micheal Bibbins.

She also attends New Life Ministries, Inc in Dover, Delaware under the leadership of Pastor Dr. Nancy Jones.

Nyoka is a native of Painter, Virginia. She currently resides in Dover, Delaware. She attended Delaware Technical Community College in Georgetown, Delaware where she obtained a degree in nursing. She is a proud mother and grandmother.

Contact Information:

Email: nyokahendricksministries@gmail.com
Facebook: Nyoka Hendricks
Instagram: Nyoka Hendricks
Periscope: Nyoka Hendricks

My Wrong Can Be Made Right

Apostle Denzel Lewis

"Denzel," a voice from heaven said. "I am God and I am changing the places where you shall settle. I am causing your feet to match my glory and I will accept nothing less than that," said the Lord. "What I speak so shall you. What I do so shall you. I am causing you to breathe, walk, talk, nothing but my Glory. My glory is over your life," said the Lord.

God can right your wrong is definitely true. Growing up was terrible, at least so I thought, until the master stepped in.

Lord, where shall I begin? "Get over here," "Pull your pants down," "Bend over," beatings after beatings, tears after tears—my life was just being beat away by people who said they loved me, but love was shown a different way. There was never a time when I came home and I did not have a beating. Sometimes, or mostly all the time, it was for something that I did not even do. The tears, the pain, the suffering, the place where I just did not understand; I saw this way of love so much that I thought this was the way to love.

Anger, bitterness, strife and so much hatred built up in my life. This was soon to be the new lifestyle that I would become accustomed to and that would do what I never thought it would do. Frame my way to love. The fact that I saw this so much was the reason why this was the way I responded and violence was one of my "Love Languages". If I wasn't beating someone or yelling at someone or fighting someone, then I did not love them.

Going down a spiral really fast, the system started to grab me and I did not realize what I was walking into. My life had just shifted. After giving up on the foster care system, jumping from shelter to shelter, home to home, this was now the way my life was going to be. I literally did not love anyone and I hated the world. Not having a father or a mother in my life was depressing. My mom was in and out of prison and inconsistent in our lives. My dad and I just didn't know what happened and did not care to know. She left us and never came back to even see if we were OK.

All my life I was told that I would preach and I was anointed; however, at this time I could not see it and honestly I did not understand why in the hell God would want someone like me. Crap! I'm hurting, I'm bitter, I'm abandoned, I'm rejected, I battle with identity, and on top of that, literally no one accepted us.

After years in the system, God sent an angel to take me in and call me their own. Even in that I still battled between the healed man and the accepted man! At this point, I was just a man who accepted this life. I wasn't healed, I just accepted it. So now I was a man who was operating with the fact that I would just accept what was being done and move on in life, but this was a terrible thing to do, I was headed for disaster.

Sometimes in life we end up in situations we can't change. This doesn't mean you approve of the situation, are giving up, or that it isn't painful. You are still allowed to feel however you feel, but by emotionally well-adjusted person is a huge threat to your mind; it doesn't want you to be happy. It wants you to deal with the past, but you don't have to. When all you want to be is happy but you continue to listen to the mind, who wants the exact opposite for you, is a monster and a trick of the enemy, you have to deal with it or you will continue to fall!

Doing things the mind way, holding on to the beliefs it wants you to hold on to, will make it very hard to manifest the things that God has for you. It is time to adjust your crown and walk in the light. There is so much that Dad has in store for you, but your mind wants to keep you in prison. I want to encourage you today that there are strategies from heaven that God will download and get to you that will blow your mind and you will not even believe it. As a result, you will feel different. You will look different and you will see everything that you have been missing from day one, see there is a higher power that is greater than the power of the enemy. What the enemy wants to do is confuse you and make you feel as if you cannot tap into the sources that God has for you. Can I suggest to you that you tap into the Kingdom of God and walk into your purpose?

If you are constantly not doing things you know would help you, if you are continuing to fight the enemy yourself without the help of God, you are in a losing battle; your mind is set up to kill steal and destroy your destiny. Get a grip on your mind. Hang on to the altar of salvation and do what is necessary to push yourself to the next level.

The change is scary, but this is what you have been waiting for. This is the newness that you have been crying at night for; this is the newness that you have been complaining about; this is the newness that you have been wanting all of your life. This is the new season where you walk into the fullness of God. Do not be afraid; grab your mind back and step up. Hold your head up. Hold your head high to dry your tears. It will be over in the morning. Weeping may endure a for a night, but joy comes in the morning.

All the 'good' things we want may come with things we don't. If you think finding a replacement is good enough for you I will ask that you stop now. There is no replacement that can fill the void other than the Holy Spirit. He's a keeper. He's a comforter and he was shielding you from every attack that the enemy brings against your mind.

If you try to make a change and 'fail' then there is a reason why you fail because you did it on your own, making changes on your own rather than seeking the power of the Holy Spirit.

We may not feel great, we may not love, we may not feel accepted, but trust me; there is acceptance in the power of God. Even when you do not feel accepted or even when you feel broken God is the ultimate healer—grab His phone.

Your mind is your most dangerous excuse. If you allow it to continue to develop excuses for you, then you will never walk into the right area that God has for you. Do you know how many times we make excuses for why we cannot do what we do, why we cannot be successful, why we cannot survive in life? Think about it. It's ultimately connected to the mind; you have to make sure that your mind is in the right place.

The problem is our mind thinks something is too hard or uncomfortable to do and sometimes when our mind feels like it's uncomfortable or it's too hard to do, we settle in just that, but I'm speaking to about 1000 readers who will read this and who will understand that you have to get your mind under control.

Can I tell you today that you are acceptable, you are above, and you are never beneath? You are exactly who God called you to do, what God told you to do, and when you walk into that you are not abandoned, you are not rejected. You are not left out. You are not a castaway. You are not a reject; you are a product of the Holy Spirit.

Is it hard to stop living outside in and not letting your feelings be determined by the kingdom of darkness? Yes, but let me say this to you today. The Lord said, "Take my yoke and lean upon me. I will give you rest." It is easier with the Holy Spirit than it is to be by yourself. If we don't really change inside, if we don't start doing things differently, our life isn't really going to change and start moving in the direction we want it to go. If we settle, if we decide not to make a change, if we decide not to be different, then we are setting ourselves up for failure.

It's hard to make some decisions in our life that would better us because of our emotions, because of our love, because of our ways, because of our heart, but we have to push our heart aside and tap into exactly what God wants for us. Whenever we experience the mysteries of heaven, whenever we experience the mysteries of God, we understand that nothing and no one can ever take our place in the Kingdom of God.

We Have to Make a Choice! Before, life handed us any kinds of cards that we did not know were going to be dealt us. We had no choice. But from today, once we came into existence, we have a choice. The failure to make that choice is terrible and it is a mindset that you do not want to develop. Make the choice to change; make the decision to change; take the step to change; take the initiative to change. Everything is going to work for those who love God. All things work together for the good of them that love the Lord.

Nobody makes that decision for us. We choose if we want to live; we choose if we want to survive; we choose if we can make it. We choose if we can be determined, so brothers and sisters, queens, and kings, step into a posture of determination; step into a posture of willingness and do what's needed for the Kingdom of God. I suggest to you today that you make every change that will literally alter the itinerary of your life. Make the devil mad as hell by stepping into a room where people look at you differently and don't even recognize you because the glory of God rests upon your life. God can right your wrongs. This is your story today. Put a pin in the old story, put a period at the end of the old story and make a change for what is needed in this time and in this season.

These changes do not happen overnight, but it will start to change in your mind as quickly as you go to bed and wake up the next morning. You might not see the natural results in the physical, but your mind has changed, and if your mind has changed it develops your wheel to make your life changed. I encourage you today. Let your mind change your world.

Apostle Denzel's Acknowledgements:

I am feeling incredibly grateful and humbled by the fact that God has chosen me for a special purpose in this life. I want to take a moment to express my deepest gratitude towards Dr. Natasha Bibbins for presenting me with a wonderful opportunity that has allowed me to grow and thrive. Furthermore, I am immensely thankful to Latrice Morton for continually motivating and inspiring me to push beyond my limits and achieve greatness. Their unwavering support and encouragement have been instrumental in my journey towards success, and I truly cherish the impact they have had on my life. In this moment of reflection, I am reminded of the importance of surrounding oneself with positive influences and mentors who help us realize our full potential. I am truly blessed to have such amazing individuals by my side, guiding and uplifting me every step of the way.

Apostle Denzel Lewis

Apostle Denzel Lewis, born on December 23, 1990, who is the founder and pastor of the WAVE Church, Texas, embodies a profound connection with God as he is often described as a man after God's own heart. His spiritual journey began at a young age, where his unwavering faith and commitment to serving others set him apart. Throughout his life, Apostle Lewis has demonstrated immense compassion, wisdom, and humility, guiding those around him towards a deeper understanding of their faith.

Drawing inspiration from biblical teachings and personal experiences, Apostle Lewis has devoted himself to spreading love and hope to all who cross his path. His genuine care for others shines through in his every action as he selflessly ministers to the needs of his community. Through his powerful sermons and heartfelt prayers, Apostle Lewis touches the hearts of many, leading them towards spiritual enlightenment and personal growth.

Apostle Denzel Lewis's influence extends far beyond the walls of a church as he actively engages in charitable works and community outreach programs. His dedication to improving the lives of those in need reflects his unwavering commitment to living out God's teachings. Whether through feeding the hungry, comforting the grieving, or providing guidance to the lost, Apostle Lewis's impact is immeasurable, leaving a lasting legacy of faith and compassion.

As a beacon of light in a world filled with uncertainty, Apostle Denzel Lewis continues to inspire others to walk in the path of righteousness and embrace the love of God. His profound connection with divinity serves as a reminder of the transformative power of faith and the enduring grace of God's love. Through his words and actions, Apostle Lewis encourages others to seek a deeper spiritual connection and to strive towards a life filled with purpose, empathy, and divine guidance.

just accepting it, I was dying slowly. I did not heal; I accepted it but did not heal. I continued to give the problem power over me and I could not begin to move forward.

So many thoughts of shame, guilt, and anxiety had me dealing with negative thoughts or events that took place that just messed me up all the way.

I had to take a moment and realize I was fighting against myself. At first, I could not spot this, but there were a lot of things that I saw but ignored. If you're feeling bitter or resentful, wishing things were different, or thinking about how life isn't fair, you might be fighting against yourself. This is the place God wants us to fix. I had to fix this for my children and all. And ultimately myself. I chose myself and now I can breathe. Every day I kept reminding myself I cannot change what has happened. Before I could make peace with life, I had to acknowledge that I was going to live and that I was going to be just fine. It was challenging and painful, and step by step it hurt and it messed me up, but I kept pushing. What you can and can't control,

God will wrong your right.

Buckle down and confront what it is. I was still angry, scared, overwhelmed, and lonely but that was OK. I accepted that reality included everything that I was feeling. When you accept these feelings and let yourself experience them without any judgment, you can work through them in the way that God desires for them to work! I had to know that all things work for the good of them that love the Lord.

Even if you're still struggling to fully accept reality, think about what it would look like if you did. After you have suffered God has a greater blessing coming with your name on it. Understanding the fact that you cannot change what's happening and what has happened can help you to actually shift into your purpose!

When the spirit of stressing and overwhelming begins to bomb you, relax and breathe. Get rid of all those thoughts that try to trap you and try to keep you in that place. I fought this and I did it for years; it had me in and out of jail, broken relationships, and all because my mind was always everywhere and I was never satisfied with one place. Settle your spirit and settle your mind and allow God to do what He does. Try deep-breathing exercises or getting a massage, do something; but I guarantee that your breakthrough is right around the corner.

Every day I spoke into my life as if my parents were speaking into me. "Denzel, you are powerful and there is nobody like you." I told myself this daily and nothing was going to change this about me. These are things that constantly remind me of that different way to live and all. I knew that there was more to life.

Let me take a stance on a few things that we have been customers of for all of our lives. Yes, I said customers because we have bought into these lies:

It is what it is. No, change that: "It is NOT WHAT IT IS." I'm not that and I bind that up in the name of Jesus!

I can't change what has already happened. No—yes, you can.

I can accept things the way they are. No, they don't have to be the way they are.

All these lies that we bought we can change; we do not have to accept it. Make a change today!

If it helps, write new affirmations statements on sticky notes and put them in places where you will see them multiple times a day and every day of the week. King/Queen, you don't have to accept that, and you are not that!

Know that it takes constant reminders every day. Feed your spirit man through the Word of God and don't allow any other spirits to cripple what God has said. Don't get down on yourself if you don't master this immediately. Start by trying it out once a week or something of this nature when you're stuck in traffic or even on a plane headed out of the country. By practicing this every day, it will be easier to use as a reminder when bigger, tougher challenges come your way—there is nothing God cannot do!

Now, I do understand that words are power and the "Universe" has taught us a lot of things. But can I tell you I do not believe in the "Universe"? I believe in the power of God! He teaches us all things. The fact that you are OK with what's happening. Is not OK. The biggest misunderstanding about acceptance is that it means that we're OK with the thing we're accepting. We have to honestly look at this because this means that we've somehow gotten comfortable with a thing that we honestly don't want. You know you don't want it so to stop saying that you are OK with it. You are not required to be OK with what you're going through, but you have the ability to change it.

See, when you step into acceptance it means you stop trying to change it. I need people who will not stop. Every day you should wake up and declare that you will not stop! You are going to change this every day until you shape your life with the ways of the Holy Spirit. When you walk in acceptance, you say you agree that this situation will never go away. And all you do is cover it up. Ever wonder how many people walk around covered up? That's deep and that's a big thing to ponder on for a sec. If we had 100 people standing in front of us, at least 60 of them would be covered up by acceptance. That's over half!

Jesus wants us to fix this and make it right. When we accept things, we automatically fail. I refuse to fail! If we are children of God, we understand we don't accept anything; we accept only what God has for us! Acceptance of the kingdom of darkness is for the ones that are willing to settle. Don't fall into that trap. It is time for those who have the strength to face the truth and stop denying it. It can be, in fact, a first step in a process of genuine success and movement and shifting into God's purpose for your life.

Your mind is so important! The mind serves us well in so many ways, but we have to make sure that our mind doesn't kill us! It has no power, but it is constantly trying to dominate, which in final results does nothing more than sabotage us and slow us down and make things so much harder than they have to be. Breaking away from the mind is a challenge all by itself. That's why the Word says, "The mind that is in Jesus let it be in us!" The mind will fight until it gets all the stuff it wants so badly, that it feels so miserable without. Jesus keeps our minds in place. If you don't keep your mind in Jesus, your happiness will be threatened. Being a happy, mentally healthy,

Shattered Innocence: A Girl's Journey through Detroit's Shadows

Tanisha Bowman

A Tale of Loss, Resilience, and Redemption in the Heart of the Motor City

Synopsis:

In the gritty streets of Detroit, where shadows loom large and hope flickers dimly, a young girl's world is shattered when her mother succumbs to the deadly grip of drugs. Overnight, the familiar warmth of her mother's love turns cold, replaced by the harsh reality of addiction and abandonment. Left to navigate the treacherous path of adolescence alone, she struggles to find her footing amidst the chaos of her crumbling world.

My name is Tanisha and my journey through life began in the heart of Detroit's toughest neighborhoods. From an early age, I learned that survival was not guaranteed, and trust was a luxury I could not afford. At just eight years old, my world turned upside down when my mother's battle with drugs consumed her. She was my best friend, my confidante, but as addiction tightened its grip, she slipped away, leaving me to navigate the harsh realities of life alone.

Overnight, the warmth of my mother's love turned cold, replaced by the suffocating embrace of the streets and the numbing haze of drugs. Our home, once filled with laughter and love, became a battleground of empty promises and shattered dreams.

As the days stretched into weeks and the weeks into months, I felt myself shrinking beneath the weight of abandonment. No longer under the protective gaze of my mother's affection, I struggled to find my place in a world that seemed determined to swallow me whole.

With each passing day, my confidence waned and I questioned my own worth. The hunger in my belly mirrored the emptiness in my heart and I longed for the attention of the one person who mattered most. But as the shadows deepened, so did the chaos. The once-steady stream of men in and out of our home became a revolving door, each one bringing temporary solace but leaving behind a trail of brokenness and despair.

It was not until I turned twelve that I found the courage to break free from the cycle of dysfunction that had consumed my life. With tears streaming down my cheeks, I packed my bags and left behind the only home I had ever known, seeking refuge with my grandmother in Georgia. But as I crossed state lines, leaving behind the familiar chaos of Detroit, I found myself entering uncharted territory. Georgia was a world apart, filled with unfamiliar faces and foreign landscapes. And yet, the ache in my heart remained unchanged, a constant reminder of the love and attention I so desperately craved.

In my naivety, I fell prey to the same cycles of dysfunction that had plagued my mother's life. I sought validation in the arms of boys who offered fleeting affection but left me feeling more lost and alone than ever before. I thank God that my grandparents never gave up on me.

As I stumbled through adolescence, I unwittingly walked the same path as those who came before me, falling victim to the generational curses that threatened to consume my future. But even in my darkest moments, a glimmer of hope remained. With each new day came the opportunity for redemption, for a chance to break free from the chains of the past and forge a new path forward.

And so, with determination in my heart and fire in my soul, I set out to rewrite the story of my life, to reclaim my worth and chart a course toward a brighter tomorrow.

Lost in the Wilderness

As my dad drove me into the sweltering heat of Georgia, I hoped for a fresh start, a chance to leave behind the pain and chaos of my past. But little did I know the road ahead would be anything but easy.

At fifteen, I found myself pregnant, my dreams of finishing high school shattered in an instant. The weight of responsibility bore down on me, pushing me further into the darkness of addiction and despair. Recreational drugs became my escape, alcohol my solace, as I struggled to drown out the relentless whispers of doubt and fear.

By the time I turned twenty, I was a mother of two, my second child born into a world of uncertainty and instability. And yet, amidst the chaos, there were moments of unexpected grace. At twenty four, I made the decision to adopt my younger brother, offering him a chance at a better life than the one I had known. But even as I tried to find my footing as a mother and caregiver, I found myself caught in a vicious cycle of incarceration and release. Jail became a familiar backdrop to my life, a constant reminder of the mistakes I could not seem to outrun.

As I struggled to make ends meet with a meager job, I could not help but wonder if this was all life had to offer. Was I destined to spend my days scraping by, forever searching for love and acceptance in all the wrong places?

In the darkest moments of my despair, I questioned whether God had a plan for my life. Did He see me, hear me, care about the struggles I faced? Or was I destined to wander aimlessly through the wilderness, forever lost and alone? But even as I grappled with these doubts, a small voice whispered in the depths of my soul, urging me to hold on, to keep fighting, to believe that better days lay ahead. And so, with a glimmer of hope in my heart, I pressed on, determined to find my way out of the wilderness and into the light of a brighter tomorrow.

Amidst the chaos of my life, a flicker of hope emerged in an unexpected place. I met a friend whose parents invited me to church. While their invitation held the promise of redemption and salvation, I found myself drawn back to the familiarity of the streets, where the rush of adrenaline and the thrill of danger offered a temporary reprieve from my troubles.

A New Foundation

As I approached my thirties, I never imagined that meeting my boyfriend would mark the beginning of a profound transformation in my life. Our relationship seemed like a breath of fresh air, a alone than ever before. I thank God that my grandparents never gave up on me.

As I stumbled through adolescence, I unwittingly walked the same path as those who came before me, falling victim to the generational curses that threatened to consume my future. But even in my darkest moments, a glimmer of hope remained. With each new day came the opportunity for redemption, for a chance to break free from the chains of the past and forge a new path forward.

And so, with determination in my heart and fire in my soul, I set out to rewrite the story of my life, to reclaim my worth and chart a course toward a brighter tomorrow.

Lost in the Wilderness

As my dad drove me into the sweltering heat of Georgia, I hoped for a fresh start, a chance to leave behind the pain and chaos of my past. But little did I know the road ahead would be anything but easy.

At fifteen, I found myself pregnant, my dreams of finishing high school shattered in an instant. The weight of responsibility bore down on me, pushing me further into the darkness of addiction and despair. Recreational drugs became my escape, alcohol my solace, as I struggled to drown out the relentless whispers of doubt and fear.

By the time I turned twenty, I was a mother of two, my second child born into a world of uncertainty and instability. And yet, amidst the chaos, there were moments of unexpected grace. At twenty-four, I made the decision to adopt my younger brother, offering him a chance at a better life than the one I had known. But even as I tried to find my footing as a mother and caregiver, I found myself caught in a vicious cycle of incarceration and release. Jail became a familiar backdrop to my life, a constant reminder of the mistakes I could not seem to outrun.

As I struggled to make ends meet with a meager job, I could not help but wonder if this was all life had to offer. Was I destined to spend my days scraping by, forever searching for love and acceptance in all the wrong places?

In the darkest moments of my despair, I questioned whether God had a plan for my life. Did He see me, hear me, care about the struggles I faced? Or was I destined to wander aimlessly through the wilderness, forever lost and alone? But even as I grappled with these doubts, a small voice whispered in the depths of my soul, urging me to hold on, to keep fighting, to believe that better days lay ahead. And so, with a glimmer of hope in my heart, I pressed on, determined to find my way out of the wilderness and into the light of a brighter tomorrow.

Amidst the chaos of my life, a flicker of hope emerged in an unexpected place. I met a friend whose parents invited me to church. While their invitation held the promise of redemption and salvation, I found myself drawn back to the familiarity of the streets, where the rush of adrenaline and the thrill of danger offered a temporary reprieve from my troubles.

A New Foundation

As I approached my thirties, I never imagined that meeting my boyfriend would mark the beginning of a profound transformation in my life. Our relationship seemed like a breath of fresh air, a glimmer of hope amidst the chaos that had defined so much of my past. We married after dating for a year.

But as we delved deeper into our relationship, my husband and I soon realized that our union was far from perfect. Behind the facade of social media posts and public appearances, we found ourselves sinking under the weight of unresolved issues and conflicting priorities.

Both my husband and I had a relationship with Jesus, but we had yet to fully surrender our lives to His guidance. Our weekends were filled with parties, arguments, and endless rounds of drinking, leaving us feeling empty and disillusioned.

It was not until we reached a breaking point that my husband and I made the decision to give our relationship to God. We sought out a Bible-based church, the same one I had found solace in years earlier, and connected with mentors who would guide us on our journey.

With the support of our godparents and pastors, my husband and I began to embrace a God-centered approach to our relationship. We committed to putting Jesus at the forefront of our marriage, recognizing that His way was the only path to true fulfillment and joy.

Slowly but surely, our lives began to change for the better. I found myself surrounded by a community of believers who uplifted and supported me, providing a safe haven where I could grow and thrive.

As we navigated the complexities of blended family life, my husband and I made our fair share of mistakes. But with each challenge we faced, we leaned on our newfound faith, trusting in God's grace to see us through.

Now a mother of six, I marveled at the ways in which God had transformed my life. Blended families had been a new and daunting concept for both my partner and me, but we had learned to lean on God's wisdom and guidance every step of the way.

And as we looked to the future, my partner and I did so with hearts full of gratitude, knowing that our journey was far from over but trusting in God's faithfulness to lead us forward.

Finding Strength in Loss: A Season of Grief and Grace

Life had been good for me. Despite the trials and tribulations, I had faced I found stability, purpose, and a newfound faith that sustained me through the darkest of times. But just as I began to settle into a sense of contentment, tragedy struck, shattering the fragile peace I had worked so hard to build.

First, it was my grandfather. A pillar of strength and wisdom in my life, his sudden passing left a gaping hole in my heart. I found myself grappling with emotions I had never known before—grief, anger, and a profound sense of loss. And as if that was not enough to bear, just ten months later, my grandmother followed suit, succumbing to the same merciless disease.

For me, the loss of my grandparents was more than just the passing of loved ones. They had been my rock, my constant source of love and support. They had raised me, nurtured me, and instilled in me the values that had guided me through life. And as they had done for me, they had also played a pivotal role in raising my children, serving as the glue that held our family together.

In the wake of their deaths, I found myself adrift in a sea of grief and despair. The pain was overwhelming, threatening to consume me at every turn. But even in the darkest moments, I clung to my faith, trusting in God to see me through the storm. And then, amidst the darkness, a glimmer of light emerged. My grandson, Levi, was born—a ray of hope in the midst of despair. His arrival brought joy and laughter back into our lives, reminding me that even in the face of loss, there was still beauty to be found.

As I watched my daughter navigate the challenges of law school while pregnant with Levi, I marveled at her strength and resilience. Despite the hardships she faced, she never missed a beat, a testament to the power of faith and determination.

Sadly a year later, I lost my father; it was a trying time in my life. Thank God that I had learned to trust Him! In the midst of grief and loss, I found solace in the unbreakable bonds of family and the unwavering love of God. Though the road ahead would be difficult, I knew that with faith as my guide, I would find my way through the darkness and emerge stronger on the other side.

A Beacon of Faith

In reflecting on my journey, I find myself echoing a resounding phrase: "But God, All God, Yes God." It serves as a testament to the incredible power of faith and resilience, showcasing how, with God, all things are indeed possible.

In the midst of life's trials and tribulations, my unwavering belief in God's plan remained steadfast. Every obstacle I encountered served not as a roadblock but as an opportunity for growth and transformation. My life stands as living proof of this conviction.

Lastly, I would like to remind you to speak life over your life every day.

Daily Affirmations

I Am Blessed

I Am Bold

I Am Beautiful

The enemy comes to steal, kill, and destroy; God came that I may have life and have it more abundantly.

No weapon formed against me shall prosper and every tongue that rises against me shall fall.

This is the day the Lord has made, let us rejoice and be glad in it.

I can do all things through Christ who strengthens me.

Life and death is in the power of the tongue.

Tanisha's Acknowledgements:

I would like to acknowledge first my husband Derek Bowman, thank you for being the ice in my tea. Thank you for always supporting me and taking care of our family.

My grandparents, Lillian and Lerome Hancock, the conditional love was always there for the entire family. You never gave up on me and I can never thank you enough.

My dad and bonus mom, Raymond and Kimberly Ellison, thank you for being the best parents and loving my brother and me with the love that only a parent can give.

My daughter, Sabrina Zellner, your resilience reminded me daily never to give up. My sons Kendarious and Malik, you are seeds of Abraham and God has an amazing plan for your life.

Levi, you are my sunshine, you make me happy.

My godparents, Freeman and Betty Repress, you introduced me to Christ and I am forever grateful.

My prior pastors, Pastor Greg and Beverly Smith, you showed me how to build a firm foundation, you taught me that prayer was always first and you watched me grow in the Lord.

My current pastors, Pastor Kenneth and Tongela Smith, you push me past my comfort zone and you refuse to allow me to hide my gifts.

Prophetess Natasha Bibbins, thank you for trusting me to be a part of this amazing collaboration.

Finally, my mother—Deborah Durrah—I know life has not been easy for you, but I know with God all things are possible—YOU Still Can.

Tanisha Bowman

Tanisha is a woman whose life is a testament to the power of dedication, determination, and unwavering faith. Celebration fills her heart as she reflects on recent milestones, notably the proud achievement of receiving her bachelor's degree. This accomplishment signifies not only her academic prowess but also her resilience in overcoming obstacles.

Tanisha's journey extends beyond academia. As a successful business owner, ranking in the top 0.1% of her company with over 3,500 business partners, she embodies the spirit of entrepreneurship and determination. Additionally, she is a three-time co-author, empowerment coach, and motivational speaker, using her platform to inspire others to overcome challenges through faith and resilience.

At the core of Tanisha's mission is **BrokeCan**, her organization empowering women to embrace their potential and pursue their dreams. Through initiatives like the You Still Can podcast, she provides a platform for women to share testimonies and inspire others to trust in God's plan.

But Tanisha's journey doesn't stop there. She recently embarked on a new venture, assisting her pastors in launching a new church. This endeavor reflects her unwavering commitment to spreading hope and faith to a wider audience.

Tanisha finds immense pride in her daughter's achievements as well. Despite becoming a mother at a young age, her daughter has thrived and is now a successful attorney, a testament to her resilience.

Grounded in her belief in manifestation and the power of affirmations, Tanisha remains steadfast in her mission to inspire and uplift others. Through her words, actions, and unwavering faith, she leaves an indelible mark on those she encounters, reminding them that with God, all things are possible. Her purpose is clear: to share her testimony worldwide, using her social media platform to inspire and encourage others, affirming that giving up is not an option—You Still CAN.

Tanisha would love to connect with you!

YouTube- You Still Can-Tanisha Bowman
FB-Tanisha Bowman
IG-Tanisha Bowman
Tanishabowman.com

Overcoming the Darkness of Depression to Becoming a Beacon of Light as a Life Transformation Coach

Dr. Monica Floyd

Synopsis:

Step into a world of empowerment and inspiration with the transformative journey of Dr. Monica Floyd who conquered the depths of depression to emerge as a radiant beacon of light. Join her as she navigates the shadows of despair with courage and resilience, ultimately discovering her calling as a life transformation coach. Through her story, witness the transformative power of self-discovery, inner strength, and unwavering determination that will persuade you to unlock your potential and embark on a journey of self-discovery and growth.

Confronting the Shadows of Depression

There were times when I found myself in the grips of darkness, with shadows lurking in every corner of my mind. These shadows were masked as despair, suffocating sadness, and relentless loneliness. It was in these moments that I came face-to-face with depression, an intimidating opponent; my unwanted adversary who threatened to consume my very essence.

I started feeling the weight of the world pressing down on my shoulders. This journey through the shadows of depression was going to be a treacherous one with many dark holes and obstacles that to me seemed insurmountable. Yet, it was a journey that I had to take. For, you see, confronting my demons head-on was my only way to reach the light.

Through sharing my experiences of my battles with depression, I hope to shed light on the darkness that so often engulfs us and offer a guiding beacon for those who find themselves lost in the complexity of their own minds.

Together, let us confront the shadows of depression with courage, resilience, and unwavering determination. For though the journey may be long, difficult, and exhausting, the destination promises healing, hope, and self-discovery.

I found myself fighting and struggling with depression pursuing me. Relationships, friendships, and familyships ending made each day harder. I fought a battle against the overwhelming weight of darkness that clouded my mind and was suffocating me. Just getting out of bed felt like the end of the world and the world around me seemed to be closing in on me.

It was in those moments of darkness that I turned to the Scriptures for solace and guidance. One verse that resonated with me during this time was Psalm 34:18, which declares, "The Lord is close to the brokenhearted and saves those who are crushed in spirit." This reassurance that God was near, even in the depths of my despair, provided some hope for me.

I started to read more Scriptures and began to read the story of Job, a man who had experienced a whole lot of suffering and tremendous loss. Job's story hit me on a deep level because he felt like I was, hopeless. Despite all of his many struggles, Job continued to remain steadfast in his faith; that man started declaring, *"Though he slay me, yet will I trust in Him"* (Job 13:15). His unwavering trust in God, even amid overwhelming darkness, is so unexplainable because I felt abandoned.

Despite the darkness the light will always triumph over darkness and overtake the shadows.

Through prayer and reflection on the Scriptures, I began to confront the depths of my depression. I began to confront the shadows. I embraced the darkness, not as a sign of defeat but as an opportunity for growth and TRANSFORMATION. The book of Isaiah offers me and you a powerful promise: "When you pass through the waters, I will be with you; and through the rivers, they shall not overwhelm you" (Isaiah 43:2). This assures us that God will walk with us through the darkest valleys.

I slowly began to crawl from the shadows of depression, guided by the light of faith and the wisdom of Scripture. Now I'm going to be real with you. Each day was still a struggle, but I faced the darkness with renewed strength and a deep sense of God's purpose. The journey was long, and I hurt sometimes, but the promise of God's healing and restoration kept me going.

As I reflect on that one of many dark chapters of my life, I am reminded of the words of the Apostle Paul in 2 Corinthians 4:8–9, *"We are afflicted in every way, but not crushed; perplexed, but not driven to despair; persecuted, but not forsaken; struck down, but not destroyed."* These words encapsulate the essence of my journey through depression—a journey marked by struggle but ultimately defined by resilience and the unwavering grace of God.

I had to embrace the darkness and confront the shadows of my depression so that God's light could shine bright, guiding and leading me to a place of healing and wholeness.

"Finding Light in the Darkness: Navigating the Path" -Rock Bottom

What happens when you find yourself in the darkest depths of despair, when the weight of the world seems to crush you beneath its unforgiving burden? When every waking moment is tainted with hopelessness and every night is consumed by the shadows of despair, how do you find light in the darkness of depression? As someone who has walked that path, I understand the overwhelming pain and isolation that can come with mental illness. But I also know that there is a way out, a glimmer of hope that can pierce through the gloom and guide you back to the light.

During my own battle with depression, I found solace in the words of Matthew 11:28: *"Come to me, all you who are weary and burdened, and I will give you rest."* These words spoke to me on a level that

I cannot fully explain. They were a lifeline in a sea of despair, a reminder that there was someone who could bear my burdens and offer me respite from the storm raging within me.

But finding that rest was not easy. Depression is a relentless enemy, a constant companion that whispers lies of worthlessness and hopelessness in your ear. It took every ounce of strength I had to push back against those lies, to cling to the promise of rest and renewal that the Scripture offered me. There were days when I wanted to give up, when the darkness threatened to swallow me whole. But I knew I had a choice to make—succumb to despair or fight for the light.

Psalm 34:17–18 became my mantra during those dark days. *"The righteous cry out, and the Lord hears them; he delivers them from all their troubles. The Lord is close to the brokenhearted and saves those who are crushed in spirit."* I clung to these words as a drowning man clings to a life preserver. They reminded me that I was not alone, that there was someone who saw my pain and offered me hope in the midst of it.

As I navigated the path of depression, I came to realize that finding light in the darkness was not a one-time event but a daily choice. It meant choosing to get out of bed when all I wanted to do was stay hidden beneath the covers. It meant reaching out to friends and loved ones even when I felt unworthy of their love. And it meant turning to Scripture and prayer as my source of strength and solace in times of trouble.

One particularly difficult night, when the weight of despair seemed too heavy to bear, I stumbled upon Isaiah 41:10: *"So do not fear, for I am with you; do not be dismayed, for I am your God. I will strengthen you and help you; I will uphold you with my righteous right hand."* These words spoke directly to my soul, offering me a lifeline of hope in the middle of my darkest hour. I clung to them like a drowning man clings to a life preserver, allowing them to anchor me in the storm.

As I continued to walk the path of depression, I began to see glimmers of light breaking through the darkness. It wasn't an overnight transformation but a gradual process of healing and renewal. Each day brought new challenges and new victories as I learned to lean on the promises of Scripture and the love of a God who never gives up on us.

The Breaking Point: Shattering the Chains of Depression

Disillusionment and Despair

I remember it like it was yesterday—the day I hit rock bottom. It was a cold, dreary morning and I woke up feeling like a heavy weight was pressing down on my chest. I had been battling with depression for years. My son, who has autism, was breaking windows in my apartment and screaming all night, and on that fateful day, it all came crashing down on me. As I sat alone in my room, consumed by negative thoughts that seemed to suffocate me, I reached a breaking point. As I sat on my bed in the darkness of my room, tears streaming down my face. I felt utterly lost, alone, and hopeless. Everything seemed hopeless and meaningless and I couldn't see a way out of the darkness that enveloped me. The weight of my burdens felt unbearable and I felt like I was suffocating under the weight of my own despair. I slept with men for comfort, but that didn't help. In those dark moments, I cried out to God in desperation, begging Him to free me from the chains that held me captive. Then, in my desperation, I turned to the very Bible my mother read to me all the time. As I flipped through its pages, searching and searching, my eyes landed on a verse that seemed to leap off the page at me!

Psalms 23:4 *Yea, though I walk through the valley of the shadow of death, I will fear no evil, for thou art with me, thy rod, and thy staff they comfort me!*

My God! My God! I realized that I had been trying to carry the weight of my burdens alone, without seeking help or guidance. I had been trapped in a cycle of negative thinking and despair, unable to see beyond my own suffering, and in His infinite mercy and grace, He heard my cries and responded. It was through the power of Scripture that God began to break the chains that had long imprisoned my soul.

I need you to understand that it was at that moment something shifted within me. I knew then that I had to turn to God in prayer, laying my burdens at His feet and asking for His help.

I poured out my heart to God in prayer and I felt a sense of inner peace wash over me. It was like someone came and a weight had been lifted off my shoulders and I could finally breathe again without suffocating. In that moment of my surrender, I finally let go and placed my trust in God's plan for my life.

Slowly but surely, I began to see changes in my life. I sought out professional help and started therapy to work through my struggles. I also surrounded myself with supportive friends and family members who encouraged me to keep moving forward, even when the darkness threatened to overwhelm me.

Through the difficulties of my journey, I clung to the promises of Scripture like a lifeline. I found comfort in verses like:

> "Come to me, all who labor and are heavy laden, and I will give you rest." - Matthew 11:28 (ESV)

> "Cast all your anxieties on him, because he cares for you."
> - 1 Peter 5:7 (ESV)

They reminded me that I was never alone in my struggles. God was with me every step of the way, guiding me towards healing and restoration.

As I look back on that dark period of my life, I can see how God used my breaking point to shatter the chains of depression that had bound me for so long. Through His grace and mercy, I found the strength to rise above my circumstances and embrace a new sense of hope and purpose.

The journey was not easy and there were many moments of doubt and despair along the way. But through it all, I clung to the truth of Scripture and allowed it to guide me towards a place of healing and wholeness. God's Word became a source of comfort and strength, reminding me of His unfailing love and faithfulness, even in the darkest of times.

As I write these words, I am filled with gratitude for the ways in which God has transformed my life. I am no longer defined by my struggles with depression but by the grace of God that has set me free from the chains that once bound me.

I know that the road ahead may still be challenging and there will be obstacles to overcome. But I take comfort in the knowledge that I am not alone in my journey—God walks beside me, guiding me towards a future filled with hope and purpose.

I've embraced my breaking point, not as a moment of defeat but as a catalyst for growth and transformation. Through the power of Scripture and the love of God, I have emerged from the darkness into the light, ready to face whatever challenges may come my way.

As the words of Isaiah 41:10 remind me: *"Fear not, for I am with you, be not dismayed, for I am your God; I will strengthen you, I will help you, I will uphold you with my righteous right hand."* These words reassured me that God was not only aware of my pain but also intimately involved in my healing process.

Unmasking the Lies

Through the illumination of God's Word, I began to recognize the lies that I had allowed to take root in my mind. The enemy had whispered falsehoods into my ears, convincing me that I was unworthy, unlovable, and irredeemable. But God's truth cut through the darkness, exposing the lies for what they truly were.

Ephesians 6:12 reminded me that my battle was not against flesh and blood but against the spiritual forces of evil in the heavenly realms. Armed with this knowledge, I stood firm in the power of God's Word, ready to combat the lies with the truth of His promises. Philippians 4:8 became my mantra, urging me to fix my thoughts on whatever is true, noble, right, pure, lovely, and admirable. Let that encourage you!

As I meditated on these truths, the chains of negativity that had bound me for so long began to weaken, they began to break and fall away. The light of God's love touched the darkest corners of my heart, dispelling the shadows of doubt and fear. I began to see myself through the lens of God's unfailing love. Then I realized that I was fearfully and wonderfully made in His image.

Walking in Freedom

With each passing day, I felt the weight of my chains grow lighter as God continued to work in my life. Galatians 5:1 resonated within me, declaring, *"It is for freedom that Christ has set us free. Stand firm, then, and do not let yourselves be burdened again by a yoke of slavery."* I embraced this freedom wholeheartedly, knowing that I was no longer bound by the shackles of my past.

As I walked in the newfound freedom that God had bestowed upon me, I began to share my testimony with others, offering hope to those who were also struggling with negative thought patterns. I realized that my pain and struggles had not been in vain but had been transformed into a powerful testimony of God's faithfulness, grace, and love.

Through the power of Scripture, God had broken the chains that had ensnared me for so long, setting me free to live a life of purpose and joy. I found comfort in Proverbs 3:5—6, which encouraged me to trust in the Lord with all my heart and lean not on my own understanding for I knew that God's ways were higher than my ways and His thoughts were higher than my thoughts.

If you find yourself trapped in the grip of negative thought patterns, know that there is hope and freedom to be found in God's Word. Allow His truth to penetrate your heart, unmasking the lies that seek to hold you captive. Trust in His promises, for He is faithful to break every chain and set you free to walk in the path of righteousness.

May you experience the transformative power of God's Word in your life, breaking the chains of negativity and ushering in a new season of joy and freedom. Remember, you are a beloved child of God, fearfully and wonderfully made in His image. Trust in His unfailing love and let His truth set you free from the bondage of negative thought patterns.

"The Power of Vulnerability: Opening Up to Healing and Growth"

Embracing Vulnerability Through Faith

In life, we are often taught to be strong, resilient, and self-sufficient. We are told that vulnerability is a sign of weakness, something to be avoided at all costs, never to show weakness. But what if I told you that embracing vulnerability is an exceedingly powerful gateway to healing and growth? What if I shared with you the transformative experience I had when I finally allowed myself to be vulnerable, both with others and with God?

We are taught to keep our emotions in check, to never show weakness, and to handle our struggles on our own. As a result, we can become very skilled at putting on a brave face, or some may call it a mask, projecting a false image of confidence and control to the outside world. In other words, putting on an invisible face but deep down struggling. Carrying a heavy burden of shame, pain, fear, trauma, and insecurity that you are too afraid to acknowledge, even to yourself.

It wasn't until I hit rock bottom that I even realized the importance of vulnerability. I found myself overwhelmed by anxiety, sickness, depression, and a sense of overwhelming emptiness that I couldn't shake no matter what. I tried to keep up appearances, to pretend that everything was fine, but the facade was crumbling and crumbling quickly. I was forced to confront the truth: I was broken and I needed help.

It was in that very moment of desperation that I turned to the one source of strength that I had always neglected: my faith. I opened up every part of my heart to God, pouring out every ounce of my pain, my doubts, and my fears. I laid it all down at His feet, unafraid to show my weaknesses, my vulnerabilities. In that moment of my surrender, I experienced such a profound sense of peace and relief. It was as if a heavy weight had been lifted off my shoulders, freeing me from the chains of self-reliance and pride.

As I allowed myself to be vulnerable before God, I discovered a new dimension of faith, one rooted in trust, humility, and authenticity. I realized at that very moment that God's love for me was unconditional, that He welcomed me with open arms, flaws and all. I now understand that true strength comes not from hiding our weaknesses but from acknowledging them and surrendering them to a higher power. In my journey to transformation, I then realized that "For when I am weak, then I am strong."

These words resonated deeply with me as I realized the truth they held that it is in our moments of vulnerability, when we lay bare our weaknesses and our struggles, that we allow God's grace and power to work in us. By embracing vulnerability, we open ourselves up to the healing touch of God, who can take our brokenness and transform it into strength.

Through my journey of vulnerability and faith, I have experienced a deep sense of healing and growth. I have learned to embrace every one of my imperfections, to lean on others for support when needed, and to trust in God's plan for my life. I have discovered the beauty of authenticity, the freedom that comes from being true to myself and to others.

I invite you to consider your own relationship with vulnerability. I am compelled to ask: Are you willing to let down your guard, to open up your heart to God and to those around you? Are you ready to experience the transformative power of vulnerability, to walk in faith, and trust that God's grace is truly sufficient for you? I pray that you find the courage to embrace vulnerability as a pathway to healing, growth, and transformation, knowing that true strength lies in surrendering to the divine power that sustains us all.

Guiding Others to Freedom: The Art of Transformational Coaching

The Valley of Tears

Navigating the path out of depression

In the next section, we will explore the practical steps I took to navigate the path out of depression, drawing strength from Scripture and finding light in the darkness. I invite you to join me on this journey of healing and hope as we discover together the power of faith to overcome even the deepest depths of despair.

I remember the weight of it all—the heaviness that settled deep within my chest, the never-ending sense of despair that seemed to suffocate any sliver of hope. Depression, like a relentless storm, had ravaged my mind and soul, leaving me feeling lost and broken beyond repair. It was a darkness that seemed to consume everything in its path, leaving me isolated in a world of shadows and silence.

But healing from depression also required a willingness to seek help and support from others. In Ecclesiastes 4:9–10, it is written: *"Two are better than one ... for if they fall, the one will lift up his fellow."* I realized that I could not navigate this journey alone and I needed to reach out to trusted friends, family, and mental health professionals for support and guidance. Never be ashamed to ask for help.

Through prayer, self-reflection, and the loving support of others, I slowly began to unpack the trauma that had weighed me down for so long. I confronted the painful memories and emotions that had been buried deep within my soul, allowing God's healing light to bring restoration and renewal to my wounded spirit.

May you find strength and courage to confront the wounds of the past and may God's love and grace bring healing to your wounded soul. Remember the words of Psalms 30:5: "Weeping may stay for the night, but rejoicing comes in the morning." Hold on to hope, dear reader, for a new dawn is on the horizon, bringing forth healing, renewal, and a future filled with promise and possibility.

Finding Strength in Weakness

Depression had stripped me of my sense of self-worth and purpose. I felt like a shell of my former self, unable to see any value or meaning in my existence. But as I immersed myself in the Scriptures, I began to rediscover the strength that lay dormant within me.

One verse that particularly struck a chord with me was Philippians 4:13, which declares, "I can do all things through Christ who strengthens me." This verse became my mantra, reminding me that even in my weakest moments, I was not alone. I had a source of strength and power within me that was greater than any trial or tribulation.

As I leaned on this promise of strength, I found the courage to take small steps towards healing. I reached out to loved ones for support, sought professional help, and engaged in self-care practices that nourished my body, mind, and spirit. I began to see glimpses of light breaking through the darkness, guiding me towards a path of healing and wholeness.

Embracing Forgiveness and Redemption

One of the most difficult aspects of my journey through depression was grappling with feelings of guilt and shame. I blamed myself for my struggles, believing that I was unworthy of love and forgiveness. But the Scriptures offered me a unique perspective, one of grace and redemption.

Romans 8:1 became a beacon of hope for me, reminding me that **"there is now no condemnation for those who are in Christ Jesus."** This verse challenged me to let go of my self-condemnation and embrace the forgiveness that was freely offered to me. I began to see myself through the lens of grace, recognizing that my worth was not determined by my struggles but by the love of a merciful God.

As I embraced this message of forgiveness and redemption, I had a newfound sense of freedom and peace. I released the burden of guilt that had weighed me down for so long and allowed myself to be enveloped in the love of a compassionate Savior. Through the Scriptures, I learned to extend the same forgiveness and grace to myself, paving the way for healing and transformation.

In the depths of my despair, I found solace in the words of the psalmist, who cried out, "My soul is in deep anguish. How long, Lord, how long?" (Psalm 6:3, NIV). I could relate to that feeling of anguish, of being trapped in a never-ending cycle of darkness and despair. Depression had wrapped its tendrils around my heart, squeezing the joy out of life and leaving me gasping for air.

I turned to the Bible for answers, seeking comfort and healing in its pages. I came across the story of Elijah, who sought refuge under a broom tree, exhausted and despairing of life (1 Kings 19:4). Like Elijah, I too felt overwhelmed by the weight of my emotions, longing for an escape from the suffocating fog of depression.

But as I delved deeper into the Scriptures, I discovered a theme of hope and redemption that pierced through the darkness of my despair. In Isaiah 41:10, God declares, *"So do not fear, for I am with you; do not be dismayed, for I am your God. I will strengthen you and help you; I will uphold you with my righteous right hand."* These words were like a lifeline thrown to me in the depths of the storm, promising me the strength to weather the tempest.

As I clung to these promises, I began to sense a glimmer of light shining through the cracks in my broken heart. I realized that God was with me in the valley of tears, guiding me through the darkest moments of my life. In Psalm 23:4, the psalmist proclaims, *"Even though I walk through the darkest valley, I will fear no evil, for you are with me; your rod and your staff, they comfort me."* These words became my mantra, a source of comfort and strength as I navigated the tumultuous waters of depression.

I learned that transformational coaching is not about fixing people or solving their problems; it is about walking alongside them in their journey towards healing and wholeness. Just as God had guided me through the valley of tears, I felt called to guide others to freedom, to help them uncover the beauty hidden beneath the scars of their pain.

In my darkest moments, I had felt like a broken vessel, shattered into a thousand pieces by the storms of life. But God, in His infinite mercy, had picked up the shards of my brokenness and transformed them into something beautiful. In 2 Corinthians 4:7, the Apostle Paul writes, *"But we have this treasure in jars of clay to show that this all-surpassing power is from God and not from us."* I realized that my brokenness was not a sign of weakness but a testament to the power of God working in and through me.

As I embraced my own journey of healing and transformation, I discovered an inner strength I never knew I possessed. I learned to embrace my vulnerabilities, to see them not as weaknesses to be hidden but as opportunities for growth and connection. I discovered that true freedom comes from accepting ourselves as we are, flaws and all, and allowing God to work His miracles in and through us.

I realized that transformational coaching is not about changing others but about empowering them to embrace their own journey of healing and growth. It is about creating a safe space for them to explore their innermost thoughts and feelings, to confront their fears and insecurities, and to emerge stronger and more resilient on the other side.

As I walked alongside others in their journey towards freedom, I witnessed the power of God's transformative love at work in their lives. I saw broken hearts mended, shattered dreams restored, and lost souls found. I became a witness to the incredible beauty that emerges from the ashes of despair, a living testimony to the redemptive power of God's grace.

God, I thank you for "You have turned my mourning into dancing; you have removed my sackcloth and clothed me with joy" (Isaiah 30:11, NIV). I can honestly say that I've experienced firsthand the truth of these words as God turned my mourning into dancing, my despair into joy, and my darkness into light. Lord, I thank you for the light, and in guiding others to freedom, I discovered the art of transformational coaching—a sacred calling to walk alongside others in their journey towards healing and wholeness, to help them uncover the beauty hidden within their pain, and to witness the miraculous power of God's love at work in their lives.

As I reflect on my journey through this valley of tears, I am reminded of the words of the Apostle Paul in Romans 8:28, *"And we know that in all things God works for the good of those who love him, who have been called according to his purpose."* I see now that my struggles with depression were not in vain but a crucible through which God forged a new identity for me—a transformational coach, a beacon of hope in the darkness, a vessel of His love and grace in a broken world.

And so I walk forward with confidence and courage, knowing that God is with me every step of the way, guiding me through the valleys and the mountaintops and empowering me to guide others to their necessary freedom. I chose today to change my mindset and to celebrate. I am now God's Transformation Life Coach, coming to TRANSFORM others from the inside out.

Dr. Monica's Acknowledgments

I'm grateful and give thanks to God for being able to encourage others. I would like to thank my parents Andre and the late Thelma Savage, my daughters Roneqah Jones and Catalina Floyd, my son Shelton Dudley Jr., Prophetess Nicole Bryant, Prophetess Sharon Lambert, and Pastor Dr. Orlando Short for your leadership and always believing in me. To the visionary Pastor Dr. Natasha Bibbins, thank you for the God vision and leading with humility.

Dr. Monica Floyd

Dr. Monica Floyd is an inspirational woman of God, a motivator, wife, and mother of three; her adult son has autism and mental illness. She is a grandmother, fervent prayer warrior, worshipper, mentor, advocate for women and children with special needs, trailblazer, author, and a prophetic voice. She believes that consistent prayer, teaching, studying, and reading the Word of God allows us to hear the voice of God so that lives are changed to fulfill their God purpose.

She was a Family Services Worker for Project Head Start/Eastern Shore of VA for 14 years before becoming a caregiver for her adult son. She worked as a teen pregnancy counselor for three years. She served 16 years at New Mission UMC as the youth minister, women's ministry, worship leader, adult and youth choir director, adult and youth praise dance leader, outreach, hospital, lay servant ministry, and financial administration team. She is a licensed elder and chaplain under The National Fellowship of Christian Churches and The International Christian Chaplains Association. She pressed into her purpose with clarity and launched Monica Floyd Ministries International in Maryland. She is also a Board-Certified Christian Counselor, Transformation Life Coach, Master Life Coach, Employee Performance Coach, Certified Mental Health and Psychological First Aid Responder, Seizure Training Psychogenic Seizures, Domestic Violence Survivor, Homeless Survivor, Special Needs Advocate/Support, the Host and Visionary of BRUISED BUT NOT BROKEN FB Broadcast, and CEO of I CHOOSE ME LLC. She is certified in Women's Entrepreneurship from Cornell University, has a bachelor's and master's degree in theology/NSOT, is a Doctor of Christian Education/Dominion Theological Seminary, and is a serial entrepreneur, author, as well as Momager to her nine-year-old daughter who is the published author of *THINGS I LIKE, MIA'S GARDEN ADVENTURE*, and *Hello Summer Bi-lingual Activity*. She is the author of *The Right Shoes-Walk in Purpose Not Pain, I'm Ready Prayer Journal*, and *My Prayer Journal*. She is also co-author of *Fierce Women Roaring into Purpose-from Pain to Purpose, Birthing Our Fierce Voice with Strength*.

She is a faith and purpose pusher who resides in Maryland, has dedicated her life to ministry, and has faithfully served in various capacities. She is devoted to being the voice of the voiceless and the broken through her life testimonies of ups, downs, and victories. She is committed to empowering, assisting, teaching, motivating, supporting, and propelling women to their fullest God-given potential and purpose.

BRUISED BUT NOT BROKEN is about uplifting, empowerment, inspiration, encouraging, embracing, equipping, raising self-esteem, motivation, and healing. It gives women a platform to share their heartfelt testimonies so that other women can be healed, delivered, and set free from their past and present hurt and pain so that they can walk into a better future for themselves and future generations. They can walk into their God purpose.

The BRUISED BUT NOT BROKEN MOVEMENT was birthed from the many challenges that she has gone through, raising a severely mentally challenged son with autism who needs twenty-four-hour supervision, divorce, physical and mental abuse, domestic violence, homelessness, depression, rejection, and loneliness. She knew that others are or have been through some of those same challenges but were living in fear of others' opinions of them if they spoke up or were just hurting too badly to even speak about it. Women were dealing with so many hidden secrets and needed a platform to give an honest testimony or hear someone else's testimony so that they would know that they can make it out of a bad situation as well.

She devoted herself to being a voice for the voiceless, stepped up to be the change, and let them know that they are not alone. They can make it as well. She too was BRUISED BUT NOT BROKEN.

She had to stand on the Word of God and started walking by Faith, through the hard times, and pray like never before. Every time she wanted to give up, she would recite the Lord's Prayer or encourage herself aloud, "I'm a winner, not a loser! I can do all things through Christ which strengthens me, I am more than a conqueror, I shall be victorious. He is the potter; I am the clay. I shall be a homeowner."

She celebrated the small accomplishments; no matter what it was, it was big to her.

From Pain To Peace

Tanisha Burton-Walker

I can do all things through Christ who strengthens me-Philippians 4:13.

This is not just a Bible verse, it's an actual fact!

Christ comes from the Greek word "Christos", meaning "anointed one".

In Hebrew it translates to messiah meaning, "one who is anointed."

Inside of our brains the cerebral spinal fluid that is produced in the claustrum was characterized by the word christos, meaning the oil of anointing.

The Struggle

There were many times when I tried to do things of my own accord and many times I failed. The power and virtue only came once I surrendered, prayed, and left it in GOD's hands. At the age of 16, I was diagnosed with having severe depression and was put on test trials of medications from Paxil to Prozac until they found one that fit with minimal side effects. This was a generational curse as my mother and brother battled with this as well.

The biggest hurdle of that came in the first few weeks, during which I felt like a zombie in a room full of people, not interacting because I was stuck in my own head with my own thoughts that never ended. The medication curbed my behavior and impulses and it kept me from getting angry about anything, but who wants to be dependent on any type of medication for dear life? Especially not for peace of mind! I know I didn't.

Yes, the medication did stabilize me, but I needed something more! I needed to be renewed and revived; that which can only come from the Most High GOD through our Lord and savior Jesus Christ. He makes all things new!

Now I can say:

I am no longer a victim, but I am victorious!

I am no longer a hellion, but I am a lightworker!

I am no longer bound, but I am free!

I have been redeemed by the blood of the lamb, bought with a price.

He whom the son sets free is free indeed!

I am so thankful that my Heavenly Father saw in me what I didn't even see in myself. He loved me too much to leave me and let me die in my sin.

Darkness

I was working for the kingdom of darkness and wasn't even aware of it, but my actions spoke louder than my words. I was angry, bitter, and wanted to fight all the time. My heart was full of hate and it felt good to spew it anywhere I could … win, lose, or draw. I didn't care. My motto was what doesn't kill me only makes me stronger. I enjoyed hanging out, drinking alcohol, smoking marijuana and hitting the club scene on the weekends. I was feeding the beast and I didn't even understand. There were times when I would drive home from the club on auto pilot and not even remember the drive the next morning. I would talk about it and laugh with friends.

Even through all my ignorance GOD never left my side. He kept his hand upon my life and kept me covered. The enemy wanted to sift me as wheat, but GOD said no. You may ask, "Well, what caused you to be like that?" Yes, I had love, but I also had unresolved hurts. If not cared for, hurt and pain can turn into anger and rage, which leads to acting out in all sorts of different ways.

Family Life

Growing up I was raised by my two loving grandparents. My younger brother and I depended on them for everything. Not only did they provide but they also gave us the best of everything. Some people would say we were spoiled rotten. Regardless, we were very blessed to have them in our lives.

They raised us up right, but, as so many children do, we strayed from the path.

My grandmother was a very spiritual and godly woman. She introduced me to church at a young age and we went faithfully together. I actually loved going with her every Sunday, getting dressed up in the many beautiful dresses she would buy for me.

My grandfather was our provider and protector; with him I always felt safe. I remember his nickname for me was "mousey" because he said I was quiet like one. He would take me to the local stores and say, "Go ahead; get what you want." I cherish my memories of those days. The matriarch and patriarch of our family were the glue that held us all together connectively. In GOD may they continue to rest.

I embrace the relationship I now have with my mother because growing up we were like oil and water. We could not get along for anything! She used to say it was because we were too much alike and maybe so, we are genetically linked. Like mother, like daughter, so I'm pretty sure I inherited some of her traits and characteristics.

Honestly, I've always loved my mother and always wanted her approval, but I resented any discipline or guidance she tried to give me because of her delivery of it. I felt like she wasn't there actively in my life, so she had no right to speak to me the way that she wanted to. At the time I didn't understand that she was going through her own issues and trying to find her way as well as I was. I now realize my mother has been through a lot and she has endured much. She is strong, beautiful, and a survivor. I wouldn't trade her for anything. She has taught me many things without even realizing it or saying a word.

My dad was always in and out of my life, he did what he could given the situation. You see, my mom was attending Norfolk State University pursuing a career in psychology when she got pregnant with me at the age of 19. She was very much in love with my dad so when she found out she was pregnant, she dropped out of college to come back home, thinking that they were going to be a couple and raise me together. That couldn't have been further from the truth.

My dad was already in a relationship and had a son with a young lady. To make matters worse, that lady was pregnant with their second child. Needless to say, my mother was heartbroken and even more crushed when he offered her money to abort me!

Now, my dad and I have had conversations about this very touchy subject, during which he denied ever wanting her to get an abortion. However, be that as it may, Father God had other plans for me to be here. My dad never did openly welcome me into his already made family and even to this day I have never officially met my half brothers and sisters. Whenever he came to see me or spend time with me it was always done in secret.

After years of hoping and wishing, I finally made the first step and reached out to my brothers and sisters on Facebook where I looked each one of them up. We spoke personally, but the conversations were cold and unwelcoming and no relationships were ever formed with them. That was a little disappointing to me, but it is what it is. I did my part.

My dad maintains that his wife is still very bitter about the situation and wants him to have no part in my life, much less a relationship where we could all come together.

He has said she would never accept me, not then or now. I couldn't imagine having that much hate for a child and still being with the man, let alone letting any person stop me from openly welcoming my child, especially knowing that he or she is my blood and a part of me.

Even so I welcome the relationship I have with my dad as he has apologized many times for his past mistakes and behavior. I can honestly say whenever I need anything he does always comes through for me and I do give him credit for that.

I've learned to accept the things that I cannot change because I know GOD has a plan and His timing is not like man's. Forgiveness is something we all must do. It may not always be easy, but with GOD's help we can do the impossible.

Forgive each other just as GOD has forgiven you.

- Ephesians 4:32

My Anger, God's Mercy

My Heavenly Father protects me. He walks with me, and He talks with me. He leads me and He guides me. He keeps me safe from dangers seen and unseen.

Isaiah 54:17 says, *No weapons formed against me shall prosper and every tongue that rises against me shall be condemned.*

We don't have to fight our own battles! We have an advocate who fights on our behalf. *I will be an enemy to your enemies and an adversary to your adversaries. - Exodus 23:22*

Vengeance is mine, saith the Lord, I will repay.- Romans 12:19.

When I was 14 years of age, I stabbed my uncle because he had hauled off and hit me, busting my lip, over a petty argument about the television. The pain in my heart was worse than the pain of my swollen lip! Having to fight at school for being picked on then come home to fight my family was unbearable to me. I vowed never to be a victim and to protect myself at all costs. I wanted to be so cold-hearted that no one would ever hurt me again.

It was crazy because my uncle and I had always had an alright relationship with each other. I guess it was the strain of his drug addiction and me being a mouthy teenager that sent things over the edge. I ended up stabbing my uncle in the stomach and puncturing his spleen. The doctors at the hospital said if he hadn't gotten there when he did, he would have died from the internal bleeding.

It's true that GOD gives us warnings when we are on the wrong path because I dreamed about it before it ever happened, but in my dream my uncle died. The dream felt so real and my remorse and heartbreak were genuine. I can still remember it to this day.

That dream shook me to the core, but it wasn't enough to prevent the inevitable. They say GOD looks after babies and fools and He sure did step into the midst and pour out His grace and mercy upon that situation. He spared my uncle's life and prevented me from catching a murder case. I never wanted him to die only to feel the pain I felt.

I ended up being charged with malicious wounding and was sent to Norfolk Detention Center to await the court date.

My uncle spoke on my behalf at the trial, which was a blessing. I hated seeing my grandparents and my mom in that little courtroom crying. My heart was in pieces. The judge showed me leniency and after three months in detention I was released with house arrest and intensive probation. Along with a very stern warning from the judge.

Still ignorant of GOD's grace and mercy, two and a half years later, I was violated for fighting in school and other minor suspensions. This time, I was sent up state to Richmond and served three years at Bon Air Juvenile Correctional Facility. While there I continued to fight and buck up against the officers. My first year there I stayed in a locked unit.

It was during that dark path that I reconnected with Father GOD. The truth is I finally realized He was always there. I just couldn't see Him. All the times I thought I was alone, He was actually carrying me.

There was a lot of sludge in my heart and thick scales of skin that GOD had to peel away to reach me. But I was in there, that scared little girl who was molested at the age of eight by a close cousin whom I looked up to. I didn't trust anyone because of certain experiences in my life so it took me a long time to fully trust GOD.

Come unto me all ye that labour and are heavy laden and I will give you rest; take my yoke upon you and learn of me, for I am meek and lowly and ye shall find rest unto your souls, for my yoke is easy and my burden is light.- Matthew 11:28–30

That was the first scripture I ever learned at the age of 16 and it meant so much to me.

It was as if I could hear GOD saying it to me personally! Today, my relationship with Him has only gotten stronger! He picked me up out of the ashes and cleaned me up. He blessed me with a loving and understanding husband whom I adore. He increased our family with two beautiful daughters together and grandchildren. No, we're not perfect, but we're perfect for each other. Our marriage has stood the test of time because we keep Father GOD in our midst. We are that three-strand cord. Stronger than ever!

The things I used to do I don't do anymore and the places I used to go I don't go to anymore.

The Lord is changing me and I have surrendered to let Him have His way. I am a new creation. I welcome the Holy Spirit within my temple and I keep it clean so that He can dwell here.

I thought I needed the marijuana to sustain my peace of mind and to keep the depression away, but really that was only a trick of the enemy to keep me bound. All I ever needed was Jesus! Now instead of rolling up I get down on my knees and pray and guess what—my Father hears me and comes through for me every time. I die daily to my sins. It's a process. The flesh is weak, but my spirit is willing.

1 John 4:4 says, *He that is in me Is greater than he that is in the world.*

Yes! We have all strength through our Lord and Savior Jesus Christ.

There is power in the blood! His blood was shed to save us and give us a right to have eternal life. He conquered the enemy and because of Him so can we! I am forever grateful that He saved a wretch like me. He loves us too much to allow us to die in our sins. He showed me that we all have a purpose, so don't let anyone ever make you feel like GOD can't use you for His glory. When the world calls us a nobody, GOD calls us for a purpose! You definitely can lean and depend on Jesus, He's a friend like none other! Trust me; I know because he brought me from Pain to Peace and I'm loving Him!

Tanisha's Acknowledgements:

Giving glory, honor, and praise to the Most High GOD … my Heavenly Father and friend who makes all things possible.

To you I surrender all and I am truly grateful for the opportunities given and the doors you have opened in my life.

Thank you to Prophetess Dr. Natasha Bibbins, I am extremely honored that you chose me to be a part of this blessed experience! I am truly thankful. May GOD continue to bless you and enlarge your territory.

Thank you to my pastor, Jo Ann (Lady J) McCrary, for all your love, teachings, and many prayers. I've learned so much under your leadership. You have truly been a blessing to me and my family. You told me this was coming a long time ago!

Thank you to my husband, family, and friends for all your love and support. I love you all dearly!

Tanisha Burton-Walker

Tanisha was born and raised in the small town of Nassawadox, located on the Eastern Shore of Virginia on January 2, 1981.

She is married with two beautiful daughters and one granddaughter.

Tanisha enjoys working as a Pharmacy Technician and in her spare time she enjoys reading and spending time with family.

One of her major goals is to travel the world and promote the Kingdom of GOD.

Tanisha's Contact Information

Name: Tanisha Burton-Walker
Email: tanishaburton@yahoo.com
Facebook: Tanisha Walker

I Made the Vow and God Showed Me How!

Mary Russell-Hankins

When you make a vow to God, do not delay paying it;
For He has no pleasure in fools.
Pay what you have vowed—

Better not to vow than to vow and not pay.

Do not let your mouth cause your flesh to sin, nor say before the messenger of God that it was an error. Why should God be angry at your excuse and destroy the work of your hands? Ephesians 5:4–6 KJV

Vow Definition- *Vow* is to make an earnest promise or pledge.

Setting the Foundation

I grew up in a family deeply rooted in ministry. Even as a young girl, I witnessed the extraordinary—miracles, signs, and wonders. At the age of six I would go with my family to pray for the sick; it was something about seeing people not feel that gave me an urge to lay hands and God to take it from them and give it to me. I didn't understand the power of prayer and words, but my family did, they would often have to pray over me and tell me that I couldn't lay my hands on everything because spirits were transferable. I didn't care, I loved to see people healed. At 10 my grandfather would have me sit on the front porch and read to him; I'll never forget the scriptures he said I was going to stand on when I got older. It was Psalm 23 and Matthew 5:44.

Psalms 23 *The Lord is my shepherd; I shall not want. He maketh me to lie down in green pastures: he leadeth me beside the still waters.*

He restoreth my soul: he leadeth me in the paths of righteousness for his name's sake. Yea, though I walk through the valley of the shadow of death, I will fear no evil: for thou art with me; thy rod and thy staff they comfort me. Thou preparest a table before me in the presence of mine enemies: thou anointest my head with oil; my cup runneth over. Surely goodness and mercy shall follow me all the days of my life: and I will dwell in the house of the Lord forever.

Matthews 5:44 *But I say unto you, Love your enemies, bless them that curse you, do good to them that hate you, and pray for them which despitefully use you, and persecute you; That ye may be the children of your Father which is in heaven: for he maketh his sun to rise on the evil and on the good, and sendeth rain on the just and on the unjust.*

Little did I know Grandfather was preparing me for what was to come. But as I turned 12, I began to rebel. I wanted to emulate my friends who stayed out late and did as they pleased, their parents turning a blind eye. Despite having a father who was a prophet, my disobedience led to my parents' divorce and I was sent to live with my mother.

Even in my mother's home, as the only child, I still felt the urge to defy authority. I thought I could continue living recklessly. Little did I know that staying with a friend was a trap orchestrated by unseen forces. God foresaw my future trials, yet I had to endure them in my youth.

When you're called by God and have witnessed His power, regressing becomes perilous. But in my youthful ignorance, I disregarded this. I envied my peers' freedom and material possessions, desiring a life different from the path of faith.

Rebellion

Moving in with a friend seemed liberating at first. We indulged in whatever we pleased, especially when her hard-working mother was away. But the illusion shattered when my weed was laced with cocaine. My naivety led to a dangerous situation on the beach, abandoned by those I thought were friends.

The harsh reality hit when I was robbed in broad daylight. Terrified, I tried to seek refuge in a church, only to find its doors closed due to neighborhood violence. As a thief threatened me, stripping me of my possessions, my father's intuition prompted him to check on me, sensing the impending danger.

The Shift: That day, I humbled myself and begged my father to let me come home. It was 1996, the year my life took a transformative turn.

Overcoming rebellion and walking in obedience involves a process of self-reflection, intentionality, and consistent effort.

Here are five steps to help you navigate this journey:

1. **Identify the Root Cause**: Take some time to reflect on why you feel rebellious or resistant to obedience. Is it due to a lack of understanding, past experiences, fear, or something else? Understanding the underlying cause is crucial for addressing it effectively.

2. **Set Clear Goals**: Define specific goals for yourself regarding obedience. These goals should be realistic and attainable. Start with small steps if necessary and gradually work towards larger ones. Having clear objectives will give you direction and motivation.

3. **Develop Self-Discipline**: Cultivate the habit of self-discipline. This involves making conscious choices to act in accordance with your goals and values, even when it's challenging or uncomfortable. Practice delaying gratification and staying focused on the long-term benefits of obedience.

4. **Seek Support and Accountability**: Surround yourself with supportive individuals who encourage and challenge you to grow. Share your goals with trusted friends, family members, or mentors who can hold you accountable. Having someone to support you along the way can make a significant difference in your journey towards obedience.

5. **Practice Gratitude and Reflection**: Cultivate a mindset of gratitude and reflection. Regularly take time to appreciate the blessings in your life and reflect on your progress towards obedience. Celebrate your successes, no matter how small, and learn from any setbacks or challenges you encounter.

Remember, overcoming rebellion and walking in obedience is a journey that requires patience, perseverance, and self-awareness. Be kind to yourself along the way and celebrate your progress, no matter how incremental it may seem.

Abusive Relationship

After sincerely repenting and seeking forgiveness from God, I found myself grappling with a perplexing question: why was I still enduring abuse? Has that sense of confusion and despair ever weighed heavily on you?

It's a bewildering journey when someone you deeply love turns into the source of your torment—inflicting verbal, mental, emotional, and even physical abuse. You begin to conceal the scars, not wanting to tarnish the image of the relationships you cherish. But deep down, you're also ashamed of allowing it to persist for so long. How can someone profess love and yet be capable of such cruelty? How can they claim loyalty while betraying you in the worst possible ways? These questions gnaw at your soul, leaving you grasping for answers in a sea of doubt and pain.

I, too, found myself in that abyss of confusion. Despite my upbringing in the Church and my knowledge of God's teachings, I struggled to find solace in scripture. As a young person, desires often overpower wisdom and the present consumes our thoughts, blinding us to the consequences of our choices.

Then came the breaking point. The day I caught him cheating, his rage eclipsed mine. In his eyes, I was the betrayer for uncovering his deceit. He lashed out, both physically and verbally, in front of the witnesses. The façade I had meticulously crafted shattered and the truth spilled out for all to see. The whispers and judgment that followed only added to my anguish, branding me as foolish and weak.

But amidst the darkness, a glimmer of hope emerged. I found the strength to walk away, to reclaim my worth and dignity. It wasn't easy; the scars ran deep and the pain lingered. There were moments when the weight of it all threatened to consume me, leading me to contemplate ending it all. Yet, in my darkest hour, God's grace enveloped me, shielding me from despair and guiding me toward healing.

I stand before you now, a testament to His mercy and love. I am no longer shackled by fear or shame. My scars serve as reminders of my resilience, not symbols of defeat. And if God can rescue me from the depths of despair, then trust me, dear friend, He can do the same for you. You are worthy of love and respect and no one—absolutely no one—has the right to diminish your worth.

Purpose and Vision On this journey you must identify your purpose and vision. What is Purpose **compared to vision?** Your vision statement will include what you're hoping to achieve. Your purpose statement will include your motivations for this. And your mission statement will include the actions you'll take to get there.

In Jeremiah 29:11 it states *For I know the thoughts that I think toward you, saith the Lord, thoughts of peace, and not of evil, to give you an expected end.*

In Habakkuk 2:2–3 it states *And the Lord answered me, and said, Write the vision, and make it plain upon tables, that he may run that readeth it. For the vision is yet for an appointed time, but at the end it shall speak, and not lie: though it tarry, wait for it; because it will surely come, it will not tarry.*

In my journey I came up with three words that kept me going forward to remind me of what God said and Who I am and Whose I Am. ABC is the one for me: A-Alignment, B-Belief, C-Clarity.

In the midst of these three I had to remember to SPEAK. My next reminder was S-Surrender, P-Peace, E-Elevation, A-Action, K-Kingdom. When you add all these together it means when you come into alignment, your belief system goes to another level in your faith and it brings clarification to your purpose and vision, but when you speak, it's all about surrendering your will and your way to God's will for your life. When you surrender, you find peace and God promotes and elevates you based on your faithfulness. Then comes action because faith without works is dead. Then K for Kingdom, everything must be done with a pure heart and clean hands, it's about God getting all the glory.

To come to this point you must always

1. Release control and put God in the center
2. Have gratitude
3. Align yourself with purpose
4. Speak positive affirmations
5. Speak life because life and death are in the power of the tongue

In my closing remarks, Be Encouraged, Stay Empowered and Go out and Launch into the deep and trust God that you will be the one to change and impact others in your life and community. Be Blessed!

By: Minister Mary Russell-Hankins

Mary's Acknowledgments

Dear Family, Friends, Editors, Publishers, and Supporters,

I am profoundly grateful for the unwavering faith and support that my family and friends have shown me throughout this incredible journey. Your encouragement has been a beacon of light, guiding me through the challenges and triumphs of becoming an author, minister, and empowerment coach. Your belief in me has been a source of strength and I am deeply appreciative.

To my spouse and my beloved son Lennard, your unwavering love and understanding have been my rock. Your patience and encouragement have fueled my determination to pursue my passions and share my message with the world. I am endlessly grateful for your presence in my life.

To the editors and publishers who have believed in my work and helped bring my vision to life, your expertise and dedication have been invaluable. Thank you for your guidance and support every step of the way.

And to all those who have supported me on this journey, whether through words of encouragement, practical assistance, or simply by being there when I needed it most, please know that your contribution has not gone unnoticed. Each and every one of you has played a crucial role in shaping this book and empowering me to fulfill my purpose.

With heartfelt gratitude,

Mary Russell-Hankins

Mary Russell-Hankins

Mary Russell-Hankins, an earnest Minister, Community Liaison, devoted Wife, and nurturing Mother, epitomizes a life dedicated to service and empowerment. Fueled by a profound passion for spreading positivity, Mary extends her influence beyond the confines of her church home, captivating audiences on various social media platforms.

Known as COACH MARY RUSSELL-HANKINS, she serves as a guiding force, leaving an indelible impact on the lives of numerous individuals with her wisdom.

As a distinguished Author, Mary boasts a repertoire of impactful books, including her latest masterpiece, *If You Speak It, It Will Come*. Her literary contributions not only impart wisdom but also serve as beacons of inspiration, reflecting a deep-seated desire to uplift and guide others towards transformative change in their personal and spiritual lives.

In the face of adversities, Mary remains unwavering, maintaining an unshakable faith that has been tested and proven resilient through life's diverse challenges. Her commitment to helping individuals navigate life transitions stands as a testament to her belief that everything happens for a reason.

Mary is a Certified Life, Professional, and Christian Coach and her life unfolds as a powerful narrative of resilience, strength, and unwavering faith.

Beyond being a woman after God's heart, she symbolizes Power, Purpose, Destiny, and Faith. Mary's journey is not merely a testament to personal triumph but also a wellspring of motivation for all those seeking positive transformation in their lives. Continuously serving as a guiding force, Mary Russell-Hankins impacts lives with her wisdom, compassion, and unwavering commitment to helping others discover their own strength and purpose.

POWER. PURPOSE. DESTINY. FAITH. © MaryRussellHankins

My Pain to My Purpose

Danyelle Custis

Synopsis

From the pain of Poppy to the remarkable story of Danyelle Custis. How God showed me a better way of life through all the storms. It took those storms and GOD to make me realize I HAVE A PURPOSE. As you read my testimony, remember that no matter what you have experienced in life, there is nothing too hard for God. Just like me, you may have had some struggles, and you may have had to cry sometimes, but remember, you still have a purpose.

From **MY Pain to My Purpose**

Back then, I was 16 years old when I got pregnant and didn't know about being a mother. My son was born on February 16, 1993, right before I graduated on June 10, 1993. I was scared, but I had my grandmother who would be there to help and guide me—well, at least that is what I thought because she was always there for me. On May 19, 1994, God had other plans for my grandmother, and she went on to be with the Lord in Heaven. I remember thinking, *What now?*

Pushing Through The Pain

Living without my grandmother was hard, and I knew I needed to do something different with my life, so I decided to go to Job Corps. Taking this step was the hope that I would now be able to provide for my baby. I had to decide to give temporary custody to my son's grandmother. Somehow I thought it was the best decision for Devontae and me at that time. I came into her driveway unexpectedly and jumped out of the car, yelling his name. She opened the door; I dropped down to my knees to feel his little arms around my neck. I said, "I am home. Let's get your things."

I noticed his father and mother look at each other. I said, "What's wrong?" She walked in the bedroom and, came back out and handed me some stapled papers. So after being gone two years, I returned to find his grandmother, without my knowledge, had gained full custody, and the sad part was his father knew and never said anything. The most hurtful thing that one could imagine is finding out someone you trusted would intentionally do this. She had gained full custody of our son and I was furious. I remember saying, "Why did you do that ?" I received a blank stare. Let me remind you she lived one house away. All I could think was, *If only my grandmother was here.* The following weekend, my aunt arrived home, she asked me, "Where is the baby?" With tears in my eyes, I shared with her all that had taken place. I mean I told her everything that had happened. Although it was not my fault, she was disappointed with me.

Knowing that I was hurting, she asked if I wanted to move over to Virginia Beach with her, and I said yes. She looked at me and said, "Oh, we going to get him back." So, I packed up four trash bags full of clothes not leaving one heel behind! I remember looking around and saying, "It's on now!"

A Different World

Virginia Beach, I was finally living in Virginia Beach. I was like, *Now I really have the FREEDOM to do what I want.* I was living on the edge, I was living my best life. I missed my son, but the last thing I was thinking about was being a mother. On the Eastern Shore, I was a sheltered child. I was not able to talk about life, relationships, or anything. I had to learn everything on my own. I must say I learned some hard lessons, some of them I never want to endure again and many made me the woman I am today. So I quickly turned to the wild girl.

This is what freedom looks like when you have never been free. I was free to live my life and I did it well until it took some serious health issues to bring me to a new reality. I was out of work, which led me to homelessness. Now I had nothing and began doing things that made me lose my worth. I remember going to the club and when I got back home to the hotel where I was staying, I heard a knock at the door. I opened it. There was nobody there, I knew my mind was not playing tricks on me. So, I went to the restroom, I flicked on the lights, and when I looked in the mirror, I saw a broken girl standing there; tears began to roll down my face. I started having a screaming match with God. This scripture came to my mind, Mark 4:24 "*pay attention to what you hear and with the measure you use it, and it will be measured and more will be added to you.*" It was at that moment I realized I had to want more for myself. If I did not want to do it for me, I knew I had to do it for my son.

All that night I prayed telling God I was sorry I let Him down and promising Him, "If you get me out of this mess I will draw closer to you." God showed me why I needed Him, why you have to cast all your cares on Him. I also know God did not bring me this far to leave me. I can remember crying myself to sleep, and when I got up the next day, I felt like God had lifted weight off my shoulders. Allow God to do it for you. He will right your wrong too.

Let me tell you how fast God works. All I had was three bucks to my name and I knew it was the day to get my child support and I expected to hear that $26.90 was deposited, but instead there was $4,388. Did y'all hear me? The automatic message said, "Your balance is $4388," and that moment I knew it could not have been anybody but God on my side. GOD WILL free you; that's why I am so comfortable telling my story. I know there are others who can relate to how you lived a life that was not pleasing to God but then God changed your life. God can deliver you from anything, you just have to open your mouth and ask Him for forgiveness.

In the Bible, James 4 talks about the need not to be prideful but for us to be humble. Share your story with someone by way of your testimony to help someone else because the Word also tells us not to judge our sisters and brothers. We should focus more on what we would do tomorrow. From that moment on I knew I had a purpose and had to make some changes and this was not an easy task. As I say on the THE WAKEUP LIST, if you need an example you're looking at her. I am living proof of what God can do and is still doing.

I fell so many times trying to get up but each time it was a lesson and right after it was a blessing. I began to build self-confidence and had to make some changes and fast. I found a place and I got two more jobs. I remember when I went to talk to the landlord I gave him my ID and 7000$; he said, "I just need the security deposit and the first month's rent."

I said, "No, take it all. I WANT TO GET AHEAD."

With the help of a good friend, I regained full custody of my son, wrote down my goals and completed and accomplished them. I'm living proof that every day is a new day … BUT GOD. Never give up on you. Let me leave you with this. If I can do it, you can do it too. This girl from the ES did it. Let me remind you that nothing is too hard for GOD. PSALMS 23

Walking In My Purpose

My life today shows a lot of growth. I joined NEW HOPE CONGREGATIONAL CHRISTIAN CHURCH where I was introduced to the late Pastor Michelle Donaldson; we shared so many great talks. I remember complaining about my raspy voice and she would say,

"WATCH WHAT GOD DOES WITH THAT VOICE."

She said, "You're going to use that voice to bring in those young ladies." With her encouragement it made me want to do more with THE SET TRUTH, a nonprofit organization committed to Set Encourage Teach young women to achieve their dreams and goals THE SET TRUTH was also featured in the EASTERN SHORE NEWSPAPER for its positive impact in the community. The WAKEUP LIST still continues.

Danyalle's Acknowledgments

God, I owe it all to you.

To my amazing husband who supports me through it all. I LOVE YOU

My favorite three children, thank you for never letting me give up.

The late Mildred, Grandma Major—I DID IT!

Sharon Perkins—I LOVE YOU!

My "Super Six" as I call them: Lakimmie, NaTasha, Courtney, LaQuita, Brandy, and Tyshon. I love you all and thank you for keeping me grounded.

The late Pastor Michelle, thank you for your LEADERSHIP. As you would say, you're anointed and appointed—missing you.

Last of course, but certainly not the least, my sister in Christ and my prayer warrior, Dr. Natasha Bibbins. Thank you for believing in me.

Danyelle Custis

Danyelle Custis is an Eastern Shore of Virginia native (country girl at heart) but now calls Virginia Beach her home. She's the loving wife of Equan Custis and a mother of three stars, Devantae, Zahrai, and Journey. Starting in 2003, Danyelle began her career in the medical field as a caregiver, and through her hard work and dedication, she quickly became a scheduling coordinator; today, she is a committed, passionate scheduling manager for a local home health agency. She goes above and beyond for her caregivers. She goes to work so early that it's still dark outside, and that's when she gets on praise on and shares her testimony through THE WAKEUP LIST—honest, encouraging, transparent videos. The late Pastor Michelle encouraged her to walk in her anointed purpose, and with that encouragement, THE SET TRUTH was born, a nonprofit organization committed to helping young ladies.

Contact Information -

Website: thesettruth.com
Email: thesettruth@gmail.com

There's a Sailor in Town! There's a Sailor in Town

Nicole Lindsay Bryant

Synopsis:

Life and death are in the power of the tongue, which one will you choose because someone's life will depend on your very words that are spoken.

There's a Sailor in Town! There's a Sailor in Town!

Did someone say there is a sailor in town? I thought I heard the loud sound, but I wasn't so sure due to the tone of what I heard. It wasn't a very manly or a tenor voice at all, it seemed to be a very medium-toned nice voice, but the words just didn't add up, so I needed to take another look.

We all have shortcomings that don't look like they belong to the body we're in. If anyone asked about me, they would have said, "She is so sweet, kind, helpful and very compassionate," but what they didn't know was she cursed like a sailor. This person is me and it is nothing that I'm proud of but something that needs to be addressed in the body of Christ because I have seen the people we hold in high esteem, yet when things go left the world would say the words come out right.

I haven't been saved all my life just like the rest of us in the book but even while I was saved there were things that I truly didn't know and there were things that I needed to be delivered from to be a pure vessel for the Lord.

Generation Curses

I grew up in a single-parent home but a three-family house full of family. My uncle lived on the 1st floor, my aunt on the 3rd floor, my cousin in the basement and we lived on the 2nd floor with tons of cousins with their parents and within the whole house cursing was a second language; therefore, I thought it was normal. My grandmother kept her kids in Church and we all went, which was the second generation, and with all the teachings of the Lord I was never taught that cursing was a sin and against the will of God. When I look back, I can truly say I never heard my grandmother curse, not once, even living with her at an early age, so I had to question where this second language came from amongst my family.

I truly think the women were professionals and had the men beat by a long shot. I must say when my family came to visit from Washington, DC it just wouldn't sound right when the women would curse, they didn't have the sound. I came to the realization that it was a New York thing, but my big auntie lived in the Bronx and I never heard her curse and she was my mother's oldest sibling, so maybe it was just a Brooklyn thing; we were always labeled as different anyway and we're still considered different today.

The enemy has a way of causing generational curses, which people don't look at to seek deliverance because it's not what we would consider to be normal sins, but all disobedience is sin in the sight of God.

Now, back to me. I became a product of my environment and I would call myself a professional curser, yes me. I would curse for no reason at all. When I spoke, foul language would flow like rivers right out of my mouth, but I had enough self control not to curse at work or important settings where my character could be judged or tainted, and I definitely didn't curse around my mother who I developed this from in the first place. All the years of using my second language and no one had ever corrected me or planted a seed to make me realize that there was more to my vocabulary than the words I was choosing to use.

The Process

In my mid-twenties I had some life-changing encounters, which I gave my life to Christ, but I ended up backsliding. During this time, I started some new things, even a new relationship. On the way to one of our dates this young man turned to me with a very serious look and asked if he could ask me a question and of course I said yes. I wasn't ready for the question that came after my yes. He turned to me and looked me dead in my eyes and said, "Nick, you are so beautiful, but why do you curse so much?"

And the sailor docked her ship right there and all I remember saying was, "What do you mean? I don't curse bleep, bleep, bleeping...." and you can imagine the face he had after that answer.

But I can truly tell you after that day it was as if my ears had a secret compartment and every time I cursed it would get stored up in there and be on replay and I would be in discussion. Then one day I was having a conversation with some guy friends, my brothers, and one said, "Yo, I hate to hear women curse, especially when they are so pretty." He said, "It's only a person with a short vocabulary who will use such a lack of words where there is a whole dictionary they can use." I was taken aback by what he said, and he didn't even know about the question that had just been asked to me a few weeks beforehand.

Needless to say, he said all of that, but he had never said anything to me about my cursing before. So I said, "So why you never said anything to me about this? I curse all the time."

His reply was, "But you're my sister and I look at you differently."

I responded, "I'm still a lady and if you feel that way then there are other guys that feel the same way so what's up with that?"

The Sailor Has Retired

Sailing along on this ship I rededicated my life to Christ in 2002 and started faithfully going back to church every Sunday and on one if those Sundays my Pastor began to teach about how life and death are in the power of the tongue as well as not cursing and blessing out of the same mouth. I was so shocked because I didn't realize it was actually written in the Bible.

That night, when I got home, I began to so some research on the scriptures, particularly Proverbs 18:21. *Death and life are in the power of the tongue: and they that love it shall eat the fruit thereof,* and James 3:10 *Out of the same mouth proceedeth blessing and cursing. My brethren, these things ought not so to be.* I wasn't even cursing anymore at the time, but it just was enlightening to see what God requires of us. These two scriptures caused me to be very conscious of what I say out of my mouth, especially that I had received a prophetic word that God had called me to be a prophet. The word curse doesn't only reply to foul language but speaking ill towards someone else, speaking death wishes over someone because as a child I would say I hate someone in the heat of the moment and I always got in trouble with my mother if she would hear me say it, but it didn't stop me when she wasn't around.

This is the part that people don't understand; that we plant seeds when we speak and if we are speaking negative things then that's what we're going to harvest as when we speak positive things that's what we will reap because we definitely reap what we sow just like it is written in Galatians 6:7–8. *Be not deceived; God is not mocked: for whatsoever a man soweth, that shall he also reap. For he that soweth to his flesh shall of the flesh reap corruption; but he that soweth to the Spirit shall of the Spirit reap life everlasting.*

We all have to go through the process and we just never know how it will do because the guy I was dating was not saved at the time, but I was but had backslidden, but I never accepted that God was calling me to the office of the prophet even though it was already prophesied to me. It never crossed my mind that I had to watch what came out of my mouth because God was going to use this very mouth to speak life to those who were spiritually dead, in darkness and needed a Savior and I must do that with clean lips.

I'm So Thankful for being delivered from using foul language and I pray that after you read this, if there is something you're dealing with, you will be delivered as well because there comes a time when you have to let go of the things that are not like God and I'm so glad I'm retired from those things. I have been made new just like 2 Corinthians 5:17. *Therefore if any man be in Christ, he is a new creature: old things are passed away; behold, all things are become new.*

Nicole's Acknowledgements:

I would like to acknowledge my Grandmother, Isabel Reeder Lindsay, and my Aunt, Shirley Wilson, for always conducting themselves as Pure Godly Vessels by never using profanity before me as well as being Godly women for me to have a living example to witness.

And to my Bishop, Jeffrey L. White, for teaching me the pure Gospel, line by line, precept by precept.

Nicole Lindsay Bryant

Nicole Lindsay Bryant is a Teacher, Mentor, Motivational Speaker, Business Owner, Certified Christian Counselor, Prophet, and Intercessor. By profession, she holds a double license, one as a New York State Cosmetologist and the other as an **N.Y.** State Cosmetologist Instructor where the Lord leads her to minister and transform women back to wholeness on a daily basis. Nicole L. Bryant is a co-author of Five books; two of them were on Amazon's best-selling list in three categories. She has been featured in numerous magazines such as *Kish* magazine and *New Being Queen*, and on the front cover of *Kingdom Fashion* magazine.

Prophetess Bryant has also been a guest on Christian TV sharing the Word of God as well as at churches and conferences as God sees fit. Nicole is currently involved with numerous Intercessory prayer teams where she prays and preaches the Word of God in the USA, Caribbean Islands, and various countries weekly. After experiencing trials and setbacks in her own life it caused her to shift from pain to pursuing purpose. She began to give back to young girls and women by helping them to push past their pain and pursue their own purpose.

On March 8, 2020, Nicole had her first women's empowerment conference called P.U.S.H. (Pushing Until Shifting Her) with the theme: Push past the hurt to pursue purpose. Right after that, the world experienced a complete shutdown due to a pandemic and she created a platform in July 2020 for women to express their concerns and innermost feelings on a platform called Chatting After Dark. This is a panel of qualified women who give feedback to the questions, comments, needs, and concerns of the ladies who attend at 9:00 PM EST on zoom. Most of the ladies who attended the conference were requesting an outlet during this shutdown due to the healing that took place during the conference in March. After the phenomenal response, Nicole was led to take P.U.S.H. to the next level.

In August 2020, she became the Founder and CEO of P.U.S.H. (Pushing Until Shifting Her) LLC where the organization helps young girls to adult women push past the hurts, pain, and setbacks to pursue their purpose in their lives.

Mentoring has always been Ms. Bryant's passion since junior high school and in September 2020, she became a Certified Christian Counselor. Yes, she did it during the pandemic!

September is the ninth month, which represents birthing, and in September 2021, Nicole added to her title as co-author. The team became Amazon's Best-selling author in three categories for the book *Birthing the Dreamer in You*, which consists of thirteen amazing authors.

In October 2020, Nicole felt a strong passion to honor her mother and she started the ALLB (Alma Lucille Lindsay Bristow) Overcomer virtual cancer conference. In memory of her mother's passing due to breast cancer, she will yearly host this conference to recognize all her mother did for the cause.

Nicole's mother served as a nurse at Calvary Cancer Hospital for almost 30 years and after relocating to South Carolina her mother was diagnosed with cancer, but she raised thousands of dollars for the Relay for Life cancer organization. Her mother also took care of various family members as well. Nicole, who has battled with cancer herself, has also became a caregiver to various family members and friends in their time of need.

Just when you thought there was nothing left to do in 2021, Nicole became a radio show host with her own radio show called *It's Your Time Pushing Forward with Nicole*, which aimed to encourage, uplift, and motivate people whom she might never get to meet.

She was led to create and teach a course named Birthing the Intercessor in You, which was a five-week course on Prayer, for those who were called to the realm of an intercessor but needed the extra tools to be equipped to fulfill the mission of interceding for the nation.

Before 2021 ended, Nicole was awarded the Teacher of the Year award at her job for being an outstanding instructor as she pours out everything that she has to her students and the customers she comes in contact with.

Nicole continues to be a faithful servant at her church, the Greater Temple of Praise House of Judah. In February 2022, she accepted the position of president over the Women's Ministry, which was such an honor.

Nicole thanks God for Bishop Jeffrey White and First Lady Drusilla White who Nicole has been walking by her side as her adjutant for over 20 years and counting. As GTOP's women's president, Nicole will push the women to another level as they birth out more of their gifts and talents. She would also like to thank Overseer Chris Edwards for allowing her to assist with the teaching of weekly Bible study and other tasks at the church.

February 2022 was a very exciting month for Nicole; she received a New York State Ethics Instructor License. She will never push anybody harder than she pushes herself.

And just when she thought God was done for the year, after hard work and dedication to classes, homework, and reports Nicole studied to show herself approved and was ordained as an Elder in the Lord's Church by her Bishop, Jeffrey L. White, on November 12, 2022, under the Temple of Praise International Fellowship.

Nicole Lindsay Bryant is beyond thankful to God because He chooses to use her at a time like this and she stands on the scripture Romans 8:28.

And we know that all things work together for good to them that love God, to them who are called, according to His purpose. Nicole can truly say everything is working out for her good according to the will of God in her life.

Contact Information:

Nicole Lindsay Bryant
FB: Nicole NHW
IG: Nicole NHW
Clubhouse: Nicole NHW
Email: Prophetess727@gmail.com

The Facade of a Preaching Wife

Dr. Natasha Bibbins

According to vocabulary.com, a façade is a kind of front people put up emotionally. If you're mad but acting happy, you're putting up a facade. Basically, it is when a person is acting like everything is so great that it gives other people a false idea of the truth in their situation. Example: Trying to keep the façade of a happy marriage. Well, that was me!

Synopsis:

The story of Ruth is so beautiful that everyone woman wants that marriage that symbolizes something great. The internet, television, books, news, and many other examples we see give us a measurement of what a good marriage looks like. With all the great examples of what a marriage is supposed to look like, we tend to create our own lies within our own marriages. As women, we cover up our bad marriages to try to look like we are being loved like Ruth. We have two different looks, the look when we are home and the look we have in public with our spouse, and it does not match.

Well, I am a part of "the women," I am she! I was that person who tried to cover up a bad marriage because I was a woman preaching the Word of God. I was that person who was abused, lied on, manipulated, and controlled but still pretended like I was being treated like a beloved bride. As a woman in ministry, you want to be the example for other women, but was I really being a great example when I was living a lie?

When the Lord asked me to write about my failed marriage, I must admit I felt ashamed and did not want to share my journey. I gave God a yes years ago and this assignment was no different. As you hear my story, please be sure to stay for the ending because GOD MADE MY WRONG RIGHT again!

Introduction: Is It Marriage That Breaks the Yoke?

It may seem like asking a question such as this can cause much confusion because of the word "yoke." The term "yoke" literally means a wooden beam that joins two animals, such as oxen, together for the purpose of pulling a plow or a heavy load. Well, when I think about a marriage, I believe the purpose for two to be joined is to pull together for purpose even it is to pull a heavy load. In Matthew 11:28–30 (New International Version) Jesus says, "Come to me, all you who are weary and burdened, and I will give you rest. Take my yoke upon you and learn from me, for I am gentle and humble in heart, and you will find rest for your souls. For my yoke is easy and my burden is light."

Jesus was saying that the "yoke" he gives will be easy but is still yet hard work. The yoke in the Bible symbolizes bondage or burdens. Burdens yes, sounds just like a marriage. So, is it really marriage that breaks the yoke or do we need Jesus? Everyone wants to be married until the yoke becomes hard to bear. The reality is that marriage is what we make it. In a marriage, one of us can be fighting hard to maintain unity while the other spouse does everything in their power to destroy the marriage. How can it be that a woman of God, a preacher of the Gospel, and a Christian counselor could find herself on the other side of what she preached? Simple, Amos 3:3 reads like this: "Can two walk together, except they be agreed?" We got something in common is not going to be enough to hold on to a marriage in hard times.

Let me share with you how I blamed God for allowing me to marry someone who I thought was a man of God. Yes, I was truly mistaken; as a matter of fact, because of the marriage, I was now living in BONDAGE. I was so upset with God because He did not block the marriage, especially if He was not ordaining it. I remember praying and calling out the name—I did not receive a green light, but I went anyway. Knowing this, why did I blame God? Why was I so upset with God because of my lack of understanding? Or was I being disobedient to God because I moved without hearing Him answer my prayers? Did I do exactly what I wanted? Was my heart pure? Was there a motive behind me going before God?

Why did I think that the "yoke of bondage" would be broken because I married a godly man? The reason is because I wanted what everyone else wanted for me. God never told me to marry, but the people at church did. I went into church and one of the leaders said to me, *"You don't marry the man you want; you have to marry the man that wants you."* I did not know much about being married, so I wanted to learn from those who had done it before me. So I listened to the wise woman and not God. I had the worst experience ever as a married woman. I was looking for happiness in a man who did not want to be married. I was cheated on more times than I can count. There was even a night when we were awakened by a loud, hard knock on the door from another woman who thought she was the fiancée, trying her best to break the door down. We called the cops because of course my spouse was innocent and the girl was a liar—NOT REALLY. He had given the girl a ring and told her that he was going to marry her—she had no idea that he was even married. But get this; she was not the first woman who knocked on the door and demanded her husband let her in. I had different women send messages to me saying that he was their fiancé. Trying to live this lie was getting more and more unbearable, but I wanted a *LOOK* that was never there. I was living in bondage; I was yoked up, so my marriage did not break the yoke but rather added to it. However, God forgave me and made my wrong right again!

What Is a Godly Marriage?

The concept of a "godly marriage" could be different depending on a cultural belief and a person's religious convictions. If I had to give a general definition, a godly marriage would be a marriage that aligns with the principles and values that are outlined in the Bible. Simple enough, but was my marriage godly? My beliefs and values line up with the Word of God, but can I honestly say that my partner in marriage has the same values? Absolutely no. Again, how can two walk together unless they be agreed?

A marriage ordained by God should share common faith and religious beliefs. The foundation of marriage should not be based on control. We have all heard a man say, "I am the husband," or, "I am the head of this house and you need to listen to what I say. I can go where I want, but you need to stay in this house and take care of the kids and make sure that my food is done by the time I get home." The bond has to be much stronger than that and offer a sense of purpose. This brings me back to Ruth and Boaz; that was a marriage of purpose. Ruth was working and she caught Boaz's eyes because she was working. There is purpose when God joins a man and woman together. We think a "godly marriage" involves love and love only, but a godly marriage involves purpose. When love is gone, purpose will remain.

My last marriage was not ordained by God. There was no purpose. There was never a commitment and definitely not a covenant. A marriage is supposed to be sacred between a husband and a wife with God. Not a husband and wife and a mistress. That is not a covenant. If a person is committed to another person, there will be no room for another person to be in their midst. Again, not the case with my last marriage. The lack of respect and love shown to me every day had me feeling like I would rather die than remain in the marriage that was supposed to add to the best days of my life. I secretly hated my life. I had to wake up, get dressed, go to work, minister to those in need, pray for those who needed prayer—but I was the one suffering and needing prayer. God is truly a God of strength. He strengthened me, healed me, and left me free from scars. The same God that can do it for me is the same God that can do it for you. Pick up your hung-down head, face reality, and LIVE! He can teach you how to LOVE again. Please be healed from your ungodly marriage—it is okay to love again.

Preacher Wife and Cheater Husband

Hey preacher woman, I need help! I am struggling with staying with my cheating husband. What should I do? Hey preacher woman, I am struggling with my wife's attitude and all I want to do is be a great husband; but now I want a divorce, what should I do? Hey preacher lady, this lady called me to let me know she was sleeping with my husband, I cannot take this anymore, how can I stay strong for my kids? I want my children to believe that he is perfect, but this mask is beginning to break and the truth is about to be revealed. Preacher woman, what do I do? I am the preacher woman, I am she!

Wait! Crying inside, how can I help them with their marital issues if I am right in the midst of them? God, why are you doing this to me? God, I need you like never before. Emotions, I need you to step back and for God to step forward. God, there is no way I can tell a spouse to remain faithful to a spouse that is not faithful to them. God help me! I found myself in this situation daily, someone was coming to me for advice, but I was hurting inside with my emotions all over the place. Because I am a woman of God, I would give them a God response and that was to pray for your spouse. Pray and ask God to give you direction. Go into consecration—separate yourself from your emotions, from the things of the world, and dedicate yourself to God, a time of prayer and fasting. As you sanctify yourself, God will move on your behalf.

Great advice, right? Then why was it difficult for me to follow the same godly advice? Still crying, still depressed, still unable to sleep at night, how could I be delivered from my own marriage that was not ordained by God? I hope you got it; my marriage was not ordained by God. The reality is that I listened more to the cheating spouse than I did to God. As a woman preacher, I was trying to uphold an image of a happy wife. When women go out to preach, their husbands accompany them and when we get up, we say, *"Let's celebrate my husband, the one that covers me, that one that takes care of me,"* and then preach like we did not just stand on the pulpit and tell a lie.

There is a façade that a female preacher has to put up in order to be accepted. There is a stigma that women preachers carry a lot of emotions. The first time you share what you are going through, you are now labeled and told, **"This is why women should not be preachers."** I did not want to have a label printed on my back, so I walked around in bondage? I pretended daily to be happy, but I was abused. Many did not know this, but I was mentally abused by a man who claimed he loved me. He would accuse me of having sexual relationships with other men and then say I was only using the "church" as a cover-up. I would be yelled at, and I was cursed out, and I did nothing. This man would go to his family and tell them lies about me so that they would not like me either. Believe it or not, they believed him. I tried to defend myself, but they would not listen, although they knew the truth. Still to this day, they do not speak to me, BUT GOD! When God is in it, it does not matter how many lies they tell, it does not matter who believes the lies; God will always defend His people.

The Day after I said, "I Do!"

If you are wondering how I got here, let me tell you. The day after I said, "**I DO,**" was supposed to be the best day of my life, but, instead, it was the worst day of my life. My best friend was there to witness the marriage and she posted the picture on social media. No big deal because that is what social media is for. It is to share your happy moments so that others can join in on the happiness. The morning after, I was in the hotel with my brand-new spouse and his phone rang. There was nowhere for him to run to and I heard the entire conversation. Well, it was not the conversation I was expecting to hear. He was engaged to another woman while sleeping with another woman the night before he was married. I was devastated. I was mad at myself. How could I have been so stupid? This person claimed to be a man of God and often bragged about being the armor bearer for his pastor.

Hearing the conversation was not enough; now my phone was ringing because now social media posts were coming in faster than people could read them. I was being called every name that was outside of my name, and get this, I was innocent. I did not know that the man that I had just married had multiple women that he was engaged to. I often wondered why he pushed to marry me. I was not in the world. I did not go to the clubs. I was not hanging out with a lot of people. I kept to myself. Why was I a target?

Before this marriage, the Lord had me in isolation for about three years. Now that I think about it, was it my fault for believing the enemy's voice over God's? I will never forget the time a woman of God said to me, "You want someone who loves God more than you do." Well, in my mind that was going to be difficult, but I thought, *Let's give it a try.* The man walked around with a Bible, had a Bible in every vehicle, went to church every Sunday, was the armor bearer for his pastor; SURELY this must be the man. Well, I was fooled by the enemy, such as some of you are!

I was praying for a "praying husband" and guess what. Yes, the enemy heard me and sent me a counterfeit. Side note: as Christians, we miss our blessings because they do not come according to how we prayed. We ignore signs because we are taking advice from those who have been in church all their lives but still do not know how to hear from the Holy Spirit. Yes, we have made mistakes hanging with the wrong crowd, moving to the wrong area, accepting the wrong job, and MARRYING the wrong person, all because we ignored the voice of God.

I remember when I was younger, my grandmother used to say, "A hard head will make a soft behind." What she was saying was, "If you keep ignoring what I am saying I am going to spank your behind." Spiritually, this has the same meaning; we can continue to ignore the voice of God and find ourselves feeling beat down because of disobedience. Not only did I ignore but I was disobedient to God because I prayed and because God was silent I took silence to mean, "GO!" I did not WAIT for God to answer, but I kept singing, "I Don't Mind Waiting," by Dr. Juanita Bynum. Really, how is it that I was singing to God that I didn't mind waiting but I moved ahead of Him? My hard head made a soft behind, BUT GOD!

What God Has Joined Together

I know you have been to multiple weddings and heard the scripture found in Matthew 19:6, "What therefore God has joined together, let not man put asunder." Marriage is constituted by God and therefore no one should intervene to break a covenant that was ordained and built on the principles and foundation of God. I knew this, so why did I marry a man that God never intended for me to be joined together with? Crying, I said, "God, why did you let me do this?" The reality is that God gives us all free will to do what we want. The choices we make against God are not a fault of God; they are the impact of our bad decisions.

When God joins a man and a woman together, it is a blessed union. I know this, so why was I staring down in the face of divorce? I cried out to God because I could not believe that I was about to file for divorce after only 18 hours of marriage. I cried out for months, "God, I need your help. Fix this marriage." Still nothing; instead, it continued to get worse. I was being targeted by different females because this was their man. Again, I was innocent in this; I had no idea that he had made promises to multiple women but I was the one who was targeted. Even after these women knew that he was married, they still insisted on being with this man. "God, can you please help me?"

I kept saying, "God help me," but I never asked Him to forgive me for disobeying Him. It took me months to realize that I never asked for forgiveness. I was so in my feelings and emotions that I ignored what God was saying to me. Just like some of us, I got down on my knees and began to tell God what I wanted Him to do for me. "God, fight for me, you know me." Crying even harder, "God, why are you silent? God, speak to me, please. I need to get out of this. Speak, Lord!"

Well, it was not until about 3:00 a.m. in the morning that I was awakened with. "You need to repent!" At this point, I am asking, "Repent for what? I do not live with him and he does not live with me, so why am I repenting?" The reality is that we constantly marry whom we want to marry, do what we want to do and then we blame

God for the struggle. So really was my situation God-joined? When "what God has joined together" does not fit every marriage, what do you do?

God, Try Me Again

After being in a marriage that was full of infidelity, how could I ever learn to trust again? As a matter of fact, I had canceled marriage altogether. I had a made-up mind that I would never get married again. I had accepted the fact that I would be single for the rest of my life. But one night, I prayed, repented, and prayed again. I asked the Lord to please try me again. I realized that I was the cause of my demise. Not because I was the one who decided that marriage vows were a joke, but because I did not wait on God.

I asked God to try me again. After months of looking at myself in the mirror and not recognizing who I was, I finally started to recognize me again. I would write on the mirror, "I am ENOUGH!" I had to remind myself every day that what happened to me was not the end of my story. Life happens to us all. Once I was healed, God opened my ears. I say ears because my best friend lived about 36 hours away from me but we talked every day. We would spend hours on the phone, early mornings and late evening; we would talk and laugh about everything. After asking God to try me again, He did just that! I married my best friend. My best friend is now my husband.

In closing, sharing this story with you is the most embarrassing thing I have ever had to do. My encouragement for you is that you would ask God to forgive you for stepping into a situation that He never ordained. Ask Him to try you again. Be healed and delivered from your past and past relationship before you move forward into another one wounded. Wait on God and watch Him work. Don't be in a hurry to marry but rather look for love within you. Let me remind you that *"God Will Right Your Wrong Too!"*

Dr. Natasha Bibbins Acknowledgements

I would like to first thank God for all that He has done in my life. This is not a cliché because when I think about all the things God has done for me, all the ways He made for me, all the things He protected me from, ALL I can do is Thank Him. I would like to thank my husband and my best friend, Mr. Michael Bibbins, for your patience, support, and unselfish love throughout this entire journey. Thank you for always encouraging me to be better. Your famous words to me are always, "Be the best version of you," and for that, I am truly GRATEFUL that God allowed you to be my husband. The Bible says in **Proverbs 18:22 (KJV)**, *"Whoso findeth a wife findeth a good thing, and obtaineth favour from the Lord."* I thank God for choosing me to be your FAVOR!

I would like to thank my children, Mr. William and Ms. Wilniqua Battle, who have always been the reason why I strived to overcome all barriers every day. Lastly, I would like to thank every person who has supported my ministries through the years. You all will never know how much it means to me to have you in my life. I remember a trusted voice once said, "A leader without any followers would be a woman taking a lonely walk." Thank you all for not allowing me to walk alone. I love you all!

Dr. Natasha Bibbins

Dr. Natasha Bibbins is a God-fearing woman who loves the Lord and her family. She is a Wife, Mother, Prophet, Pastor, Co-Author, Author, Certified Life & Executive Leadership Coach, Sister, and a Friend. She is the Founder of Natasha Bibbins Ministries, Forever Fire Empowerment (501c3), Sisters Empowering Sisters Ministries, The Recharge Movement (501c3), and Recharge Outreach Ministry.

She is the visionary of the Walker Family Prayer Call as she believes in the principle that family is her first ministry, as spoken in **1 Timothy 3:5**, "If anyone does not know how to manage his own family, how can he take care of God's church?"

Natasha also became a Best-Selling Co-Author in 2020 for the *Dreamer on the Rise* book compiled by Dr. Kishma George and again in 2022 for the book *Called to Intercede*. She is also the author of *Recharge Empowerment* and *Journal* and *God Will Right Your Wrong*.

Natasha received an Honorary Doctorate in Christian Leadership from the School of the Great Commission Theological Seminary in January 2021.

Professionally, Natasha has a master's degree in management, a bachelor's degree in business management, and an associate degree in business administration. She is currently a student at Liberty University in pursuit of her Doctor of Strategic Leadership degree and a student at Old Dominion University in pursuit of a second master's degree in public administration.

Natasha was honored with two awards, a Servant Leader Award and the Walking in Grace Leadership Award in 2022.

Natasha is married to Minister Michael Bibbins and is blessed to have two children, Wilniqua and William, and three bonus children, Michael II, Shenelle, and Pamela, plus one granddaughter, Aniya, and one son-in-law, Harold.

Natasha's favorite scripture is **Romans 8:18**: "For I reckon that the sufferings of this present time are not worthy to be compared to the glory which shall be revealed in us." This scripture reminds her to keep pressing and keep pushing because greatness is right around the corner.

Contact Information

Website: www.natashabibbins.com
Email: admin@natashabibbins.com
Facebook: DrNatasha Bibbins
YouTube: Natasha Bibbins Forever Fire
Clubhouse: Natasha Bibbins
Recharge Outreach Ministry Phone: 757-652-2245

Made in the USA
Middletown, DE
23 June 2024